Maude

An Oregon Trail Childhood

By

Maude Summers Maple
Oregon Pioneer

Library of Congress Catalog Card Number : 93-79255
ISBN 0-9637370-0-7

Production in cooperation with Frontier Publishing Company, Seaside, Oregon
Printed in the United States of America

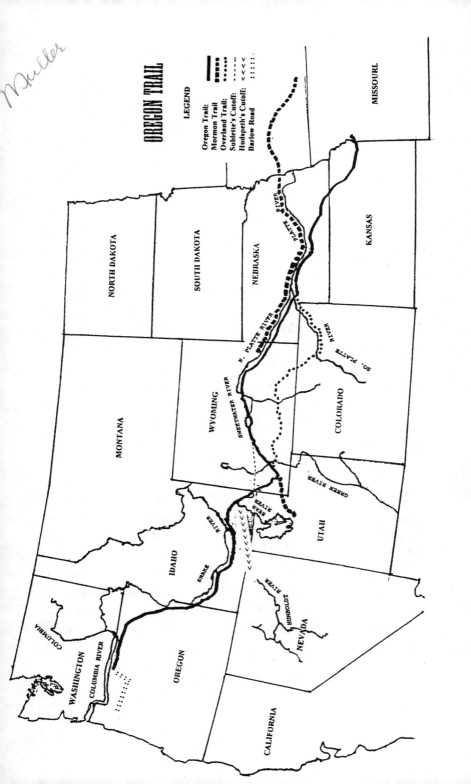

Contents

Chapters

Foreword

From the time I was around six years old, I can remember listening to mother telling stories about her experiences in crossing the prairies in a covered wagon back in the late 1870's. She had even more stories about growing up in the little community of Union in eastern Oregon in those pioneering times before cars, radio or electricity. Often the fascinated listeners were family friends and neighbors. More often they were my older brother, Summers, and me. She often said that being a covered wagon child and then growing up in Union were two of the highlights of her life.

When mother told her stories of those years, her voice, her eyes and her animated expressions left no doubt with her listeners that these were experiences she had greatly enjoyed. I believe her telling and retelling those stories was her way of trying to hang on to a precious part of her past. It didn't come as any great surprise to me when she announced one day that she had decided to put that part of her life down on paper.

Because I was involved with the editing of two different magazines around the time she began writing her memoirs, she seemed to assume that I would somehow get them preserved in print for the rest of the extended family and friends to read. I asked her more than once, as she sent the chapters to me one or two at a time, all written in longhand on ruled tablets, how she could recall so clearly, after all those years, the conversations of many people in her cast of personalities.

Her answer was that, since she was only going on six years of age when they started out from southern Colorado, she couldn't remember with that precision. But, she explained, her mother and father—my maternal grandparents—were both fine storytellers, and she listened over and over to their accounts of their prairie schooner adventures. According to mother, her parents often recalled at home with each other and with her, many experiences on their journey. When friends came to dinner or her parents went visiting, and those occasions almost always included her, part of such evenings were customarily spent in small talk and story telling.

Her parents had a goodly stock of Oregon Trail stories. Many of their listeners also had either traveled on the Oregon Trail or had relatives or friends who had done so.

Mother said she must have heard her "papa" tell his story about tobacco-chewing and spitting "Old Susan" more than a hundred times. When mother began to set all this down on paper, she liked to recall a particular experience and then put into words the general sense of that conversation. She had a fine memory for detail, so I believe the conversations must ring pretty true.

Alpheus Fuller Maple
McLean, Virginia, 1993

Preface

"Maudie" Summers was a lively, observing young lady when she began traveling with her parents in their covered wagon from southwest Colorado to Oregon. At that tender age, she almost certainly had no thought of ever writing anything about the trip beyond recording in her little copybook for Mr. Hontune, an elderly bachelor, the names of all the rivers they would cross on the way to Oregon. Thus it is understandable that she didn't pay much attention to the size of tiny settlements, little towns, and a few large cities their covered wagon passed through on the way to Oregon. She did not keep a diary. This story is a combination of her own written recollections and a few stories that she told her sons.

Believing the reader might find a bit more information on such matters interesting while traveling on the journey with Maudie, I have, in editing her story, added such facts from time to time. A few facts also have been added regarding the main westward movement trails: Oregon Trail, Mormon Trail, Overland Trail, and the California Trail. In each case my additions are marked by parentheses. The Mormons traveled on the Oregon Trail part of the way to Utah. Many people taking the Overland Trail, including Maudie's family, traveled part of the way on the Mormon Trail and the Oregon Trail. Some writers use the name Overland Trail in a generic sense, and even refer to the Oregon Trail by that name.

Professor T. A. Larson, who spent many years as a member of the University of Wyoming's Department of History, wrote in his superb *History of Wyoming*, that, "...A more southerly route, the *Overland Trail*, (italics are mine) was used by many emigrants, especially in the years 1862-1868, but also to some extent, as late as 1900...."

Why did Maudie's parents decide to take the Overland Trail across Wyoming to Salt Lake City? We are not told. They joined part of the Oregon Trail only after they had traveled across Wyoming, through Utah, and about sixty miles northward in southeastern Idaho Territory.

Was it simply because of the chance meeting in Denver with a wagon train heading for Laramie, and the invitation to join them? Or did Johnnie and Mollie Summers find it reason enough to be able to get onto a trail across Wyoming about seventy miles south of where they would have had to travel to get onto the main Oregon Trail?

Were they swayed by the fact that papa was something of a loner? Or by his somewhat delicate health at the beginning of the trip, and perhaps the feeling that there was some security in following the Overland Trail, which was fairly close to the Union Pacific Railroad, completed in 1869? Perhaps a combination of these considerations. My guess is that they followed the Overland Trail for the same reason that thousands of others did: because it was closest at hand and had proved to be a good, serviceable route.

Maybe Maudie's story will interest you to further study this saga of that great Western migration. It was carried out most heavily in the 1840s through the 1860s, but, as many historians of that epic adventure noted, it continued to some extent for another three decades.

Maudie's story also tells us a lot about growing up in a small town in eastern Oregon in pioneer days—in an era when the pace of life was slower, when ways were gentler, and there was more time for family life and visiting with friends and neighbors.

Will Muller, Editor

Acknowledgments

The cover oil painting is by Bob Golightly and the pen and ink sketches in chapter headings are by Donald A. Scott, except those in chapters 1, 2, 4 and 9, which are by Rudolph Wendelin, courtesy of U. S. Forest Service.

Grateful thanks to the staffs of the Oregon Historical Society, in Portland, Oregon and the National Historic Oregon Trail Interpretive Center on the outskirts of Baker City, Oregon, for their fine Oregon Trail displays and assistance of their interpretive staffs in answering questions, which helped to clarify factual questions related to Maudie's story and to provide some of the factual material which has been added.

Leonard Almquist, Curator of the Union County Museum and City Manager of Union, was very helpful in providing information and guiding us to old-timers to help verify historical facts about the Union of Maudie's era, which was more than a century earlier.

Thanks and gratitude go to the staff of the Wyoming State Historical Museum in Cheyenne, and particularly to Ann Nelson, a Senior Historian. Grateful thanks also to Director Mary Belle Lambertsen and Darlene Shillinger of the Carbon County Museum, Rawlins, Wyoming; to the staff of the Utah State Historical Society in Salt Lake City; to Patrick J. Fraker at the Colorado Historical Museum in Denver, and to the staff of the Sweetwater County Historical Museum, Green River, Wyoming.

In searching for information regarding old Fort Hall, gratitude goes to Larry Jones, Idaho State Historical Museum in Boise, Lou Chavers, Pocatello City Library, Wayne Rickard, Director of City Parks, Pocatello, and to Joyce Ballard,

Director of the Shoshone-Bannock Tribal Museum on the Ft. Hall Indian Reservation.

All these people gave generously of their time and specialized knowledge to verify, and in some cases to provide factual information related to size and makeup of communities along the Trails during those pioneering years. Some provided photographs.

Many thanks to Tom Hardman, journalist and editor, who took the time to review the manuscript and offer constructive suggestions. Finally, thanks to the American Association For State and Local History for permission to use the map showing the various trails across Wyoming.

Chapter I

I Become A Covered Wagon Child

Papa came into the ranch house from the big barn, jauntier than usual that spring evening. Mama was standing in front of the kitchen range, cooking supper, and I was by the woodbox.

"Everything's set!" he said. "Wagon's all loaded!" We could tell by his voice and big grin that he was as happy as a young boy.

He walked over to wash his hands at the kitchen sink. I followed and stood beside him. Above the noise of the hand pump and the water pouring out of it into a tin wash basin, he half-turned to me and said, "Maudie, we'll have breakfast before the roosters crow tomorrow. Then we'll head out. Are you all packed?"

"Yes, papa," I answered. "Mama helped me." I didn't tell him she actually did all my packing, except I stood and told her I wanted to take certain things she was prepared to leave behind due to the lack of space. I also told her I wanted to carry with me my dollie and a little teddy bear Grandma

1

Knowles sent me last Christmas.

I knew from suppertime talk between mama and him during the past few months, and in evenings as we sat around the big stone fireplace in the front room, that soon we'd be leaving this little cattle ranch papa had managed, with the help of a couple of cowboys, these past two years. It was nestled in a pretty valley by the *Sangre de Cristo* mountains, about 200 miles southwest from Denver.

He wanted to take us to Oregon country. Out there, he said, we might be able to get a government homestead of 160 acres of farm land and build up a nice little ranch of our own. He told mama over and over that the Willamette Valley in Oregon is lush and green and beautiful, with lots of nice flowers and fruit trees and other trees.

The cowboys were very nice. I spent quite a bit of my time out by the barns, other outbuildings, and corral, watching them work. But they weren't my idea of how cowboys really looked and acted. Even though I was only going on six, I knew exactly how a cowboy should look and the kind of work he does. I never saw one until we got to the ranch, but I had seen pictures of them in magazines.

A real cowboy was tall and handsome, and he wore boots with high heels and spurs. He also wore a big cowboy hat and tied a bandana around his neck. Except when he was eating and sleeping, he rode a beautiful big horse with kind eyes.

But not Sneed and Shortie. In winter they worked around the barn and corrals a lot. They often wore overalls and stocking caps or no hats at all. And they spent most of their time doing chores like putting up new fence posts and stringing barbed wire and repairing outbuildings. In summer, they cut hay. They rode their horses to herd cattle only a small part of the time, and they rode them when they went in to Saguache to spend Saturday nights.

It was still dark the next morning when mama came in and awakened me. The room was icy cold. The ranch was up about 7,000 feet. Our only heat was from the kitchen range and the fireplace in the front room. I learned later that some people called such a room the parlor.

"Your papa's harnessing the horses," she said. "Hurry now! He wants us to eat in a few minutes." She gave me a quick hug and kiss and went back to the kitchen. This morning mama seemed to share at least some of papa's and my excitement over starting out for Oregon.

I gathered up my clothes, ran to the kitchen and stood beside the stove. Its crackling wood fire warmed me while I dressed and listened to the eggs and bacon frying and the coffee bubbling. I had already noticed by that early age that mountain air somehow makes good food smell and taste even better.

Before the sun peeked up over the lowest ridge, papa had the team of big draft horses—King and Sparkie—hitched to the wagon. Charlie, the third work horse, a spare, would be tied to the rear and follow along.

When mama shut the ranch house door the final time, and we stood on the back porch and watched our covered wagon pull up in front of us, it looked simply huge. So did the horses. Papa had told me King and Sparkie each weighed around 1500 pounds. Charlie was lighter, and was intended to both ride and pull a wagon. Papa sat on the long wooden seat that rested on top of big curving steel springs on each side. He held all four reins in one hand.

Mama put one foot on a wheel spoke, then climbed up on it. From there papa could pull her up to the seat. Then she reached down and one of the cowboys handed me up to her. They put me in the middle between them.

We waved goodbye to the cowboys and the new manager and his wife. They had arrived a few days earlier and insisted on staying in another little outbuilding near the bunkhouse until they took over. Papa released a big iron hand brake on the outside of the wagon on the left side where he sat. He lifted the reins, clucked to the horses, and the wheels started rolling. Papa trotted the horses through the ranch gate. A minute later he turned them north over a twisting, rutted dirt and gravel road, more like a cow trail.

At last we were on our way to Oregon country!

The wagon was almost brand new. Papa had ordered it through the store where he worked when he first came to Colorado. When it arrived a few months earlier, we all went into Saguache to bring it back to the ranch.

The wagon looked bigger than the ranch work wagons but not much. Its shiny yellow wheels with iron rims were much taller than I. It was called a "covered wagon" because the whole upper part was covered with heavy canvas, which looked something like a half-round tent. The canvas was held up by a half-dozen big wooden bows—made of hickory, I think—and shaped sort of like a horseshoe. The canvas was wider at the top than where it fastened to the wagon's high wooden sides. Canvas flaps at each end, with draw-strings, could be closed against rain or dust whipped by the wind, and to keep out mosquitoes and other flying insects. They didn't always do that. On one side of the wagon a wooden water barrel rested on a sort of wooden shelf and was held secure by a rope.

Papa had stored all our worldly goods on the wagon floor. When mama said they took up precious little room, papa was quick to reply that by the time they finished buying in Denver all the things needed for the trip, it would be jammed.

4

We should make Denver in about two weeks," papa said cheerily. Mama smiled back, still looking excited.

She put her arm around me and said, "Maudie, this seat is so high off the ground. You must never try to stand up while the wagon's moving."

This was only my second ride in the wagon. My first one was when papa drove it back to the ranch. Now I was learning quickly how it felt to ride in it from sunup to late afternoon or near sundown. When we came to a spot where there were both water and grass for the horses, papa would say, "This looks like a good stopping place."

Then he'd draw up close to the river or creek and unhitch the horses. At the same time mama would start getting set up for supper. She'd find a level spot, get out a board we carried and set it on anything she could find to make a little table. Otherwise, she'd set it on the ground and lay the checkered oilcloth tablecloth on top of it. After that she'd dig around in the "grub box" in the back of the wagon, and get out some food.

The first thing papa did in camp was to water the horses at the river or creek. Then he'd get the axe from the wagon and take me with him to look for dead limbs for firewood. I helped carry it back to camp. Most of the time he'd make the fire, but sometimes mama did that while he checked the horses' feet or took the rifle or fish line and went out to look for some game or fish for supper.

I learned years later that there were very few good dirt roads in those days. People walking or on horseback some-times followed wild animal trails or cow trails. I also came to know much later that by 1878, a very large number of people had already gone West from starting points like St. Joseph or Independence, Missouri, or from Iowa or Nebraska. They got onto the Oregon Trail at various places along the way, depending on which state they started from, headed for Oregon, Utah, or California. The Oregon Trail and a few other trails were well-enough marked by wagon wheel ruts so that travelers could see and follow much of the time. But on the trip from Saguache to Denver, we weren't on the Oregon Trail. We'd pick it up eventually. Papa guided Sparkie and King over rough, mostly poorly marked trails. Sometimes we took the wrong turn; it would end up at a dead end like a mountain lake or a canyon or a grove of trees. Then he'd turn the horses around and retrace our steps until we picked up the trail or wagon track again.

We climbed hills and dropped into little valleys and went around the foot of pine-covered mountains. For the first few days we had the snow-capped *Sangre de Cristo* mountains in sight. After a while we began to head northward toward Denver. Spring rains and melting snow had caused the creeks and rivers to swell. Rushing waters made wide, ragged looking cracks or ruts in our wagon trail.

Sometimes papa and mama had to climb down off the wagon with shovels and an axe and fill in with enough rocks, dirt and blowdown tree limbs to drive over that point. The horses often stumbled and stopped while trying to cross. Papa would shout mightily to them, urging them on. With lunging pulls they would get us back on solid ground. Then all three of us would exchange side glances which said, *Well, we did it again.*

As we drew closer to Denver, the land became flatter, there were more signs of ranches, and the wagon trail became easier to follow. One day, after we'd been traveling about two weeks just like papa said, mama looked around as we emerged from a forest of pines. "There's Denver!" she almost shouted. What a welcome sight!

Denver is a mile high, so the weather was still cool

even this late spring day, but it also was clear and sunny. The horses seemed to sense they were coming to a destination, for they raised their tails, held their ears forward and trotted with a burst of new energy the rest of the way. As we drew closer, we could make out more clearly the outlines of buildings. Some were four or five stories high.

(In the spring of 1878, Denver, with a population of around 30,000, was the largest city between there and Wichita to the East and Salt Lake City to the West.)

As we reached the edge of the city, papa stopped a rancher and his wife in a buckboard coming toward us and asked directions to a good camping spot.

"Where you headed fur?" the rancher asked pleasantly, while his wife smiled at us.

"Oregon country!" papa said, sounding proud.

"There's a reg'lar campin' grounds which has sprouted up over the past few years for wagons headin' for Oregon," the rancher said. He gave directions for finding it.

In less than an hour we drove into a big, level meadow with scatterings of leafy trees and a clear, fresh-running creek bordering it. Here about a dozen families were camped with their covered wagons and teams of horses, mules, and oxen. Two families each had a cow and another family had two cows and some chickens. There were also a half-dozen or more saddle horses that men accompanying the wagon trains rode. All of these people stopped to rest and reprovision on their way to Oregon or California. Papa pulled up to a nice shaded spot not far from the creek. There we camped for the next three weeks while he and mama finished their outfitting for our trip to Oregon.

Chapter II

Happy Stopover in Denver

In further outfitting for our trip, papa seemed to keep his mind almost entirely on what we'd need. He had a list on several sheets of heavy wrapping paper. Mama had helped prepare it at the ranch, and they kept adding to it on the way to Denver. Back at the ranch I sometimes heard them talking about things they'd need for the journey. They included stuff like coal oil (later known as kerosene) for our lamp, rope, buckets, axe and hatchet, canvas, extra leather to repair harness, axle grease, hand tools, horseshoeing equipment, ammunition for papa's two guns, medicines, some more clothes, and lots of dried food like beans, flour, rice, corn-meal, noodles, sugar, and salted bacon. There were no tinned foods in those days.

But mama had her own ideas about how to spend her time in Denver. More than once she had mentioned before we ever left the ranch, that we'd been there for around two years with no near neighbors, so she wanted us to have a little vacation and look around and enjoy ourselves when we got to Denver. After the first four or five days, she'd had enough of following papa into hardware stores and harness shops, gun shops, and blacksmith shops. Papa did all the talking with the sales clerks anyway, and he made most decisions on those things. Mama finally asked papa to give her the parts of the shopping list that had food, clothing— for her and me—and a medicine kit. She said she'd take care of those things. Then when we left papa outside the first store he was going to that morning, she turned to me.

"Maudie, let's go see Denver!"

She knew it would be a long time before we'd again see such nice stores and little shops, and she was determined to make the most of it. She did talk papa several times into taking us to dinner at lovely restaurants and to walk us through the lobbies of Denver's nice big hotels: the Palmer, the Winthrop, and the Grand Central. I didn't remember the names then, but mama and papa sometimes spoke of them years later when recalling our Denver visit.

"Maudie," mama said to me several times during those exciting days, "I just love Denver!"

We mixed a lot of sightseeing in between the serious shopping. For a little girl who had lived two years on a ranch many miles from the nearest small town, every hour was a great experience. We saw cowboys, sometimes in groups of three or more, riding past our encampment near the South Platte River. One day we saw several Indian men with long hair ride bareback past the camp. They wore trousers and shirts made from what papa said was deerskin. I thought those Indians looked strong and nice, and I couldn't imagine their ever wanting to hurt us as we traveled Westward.

The streets teemed with horses and wagons of all descriptions. I don't recall seeing any paved streets, and

9

there were no cars in those days. Horse-drawn streetcars clanged their bells in warning to wagons and to people walking too close. I was occasionally surprised to see Indians dressed like city workmen. I saw several Indian men walking along the streets, who were dressed and had their hair cut like papa's and other men's who weren't Indians. Once two of them saw me staring at them. I smiled at them, and they smiled back at me in a friendly way.

We also saw a few black people. I heard papa say years later that a nice four-story hotel in Denver in those early years was built by a prominent black businessman.

For mama and me it was heavenly to gaze into all those store windows—many of them beautifully decorated and brimming with pretty dresses and shoes and ladies' and girls' hats. Some windows had storybooks for children, with wonderful colored pictures. Bakeries sent out such good fragrances, and their windows were filled with mouth-watering pies, cakes, doughnuts and cookies. To me, all this was a big adventure at every turn.

On our last trip to the stores, papa was along, and he bought me some heavy-soled shoes with copper toes. Oh! I was so proud of those shoes! All the way back to camp I kept looking down at them.

Papa announced one afternoon that we were finally ready to head north to Cheyenne, Wyoming Territory. There we would start heading west for Oregon. His voice sounded eager again, and excited—like when we left the ranch at Saguache.

At the encampment, wagon trains—and sometimes just one or two wagons traveling by themselves—would arrive, stay a few days and move on. After we'd been there nearly three weeks, we became acquainted with a couple of covered wagon families who pulled in a few days back with a small wagon train. They were taking a rest and, like us, adding to their supplies before traveling on.

At night they'd gather around a big bonfire, and one friendly looking man and his wife stopped by and invited us to go to the campfire with them. Papa and mama looked pleased and said, yes, they'd like to go. After that, we attended their campfire gatherings each night. Most of the grownups seemed a little older than mama and papa. One night I was excited to see several girls and boys about my age and older. I had caught glimpses of them around camp but never got a chance to visit with them since we were downtown each day, and I guess some of them were too. One girl who sat near us, seemed especially nice. We kept looking at each other and smiling. After a while, she walked over and stood beside me, still smiling.

"My name's Laurie," she said. "What's yours?"

"Maudie," I answered, grinning happily at the prospect of at last making a friend my age. "We're going to Oregon."

She pointed out three boys and a baby girl, and said they were her brothers and sister, and that her family were part of a wagon train which already had traveled up from somewhere in Colorado and that her papa was a carpenter. Then her eyes lit up and she asked excitedly, "Think our wagons might travel together?"

I turned to mama. "Oh, can't we go with them?"

Mama smiled warmly at both of us. "That would be nice. I believe papa and the other men have talked about our traveling together— at least to Laramie."

And that's the way it turned out. Two mornings later, a man with a big cowboy hat, who was "wagonmaster" for the whole wagon train, sat in the first wagon in a line of eight, and he called out in a loud, deep voice for his four mules to move out. He lifted the reins. Soon papa called out the signal for King and Sparkie. They started forward, with Charlie tied and following behind. The wagon gave a big jerk, and we were finally on our way again.

Even then, as a small girl, I felt that if mama could have had things her way, we would have settled in Denver. But she said very little about her feelings in the matter, and did nothing to discourage papa's search for greener pastures. He had so much hope built up inside him, I knew even then, for good things out in Oregon country. Papa was always a dreamer. Mama had a much more down-to-earth approach to life. And this is the way it always remained.

One of my very few memories of mama when I was a only a little past three years old was of a day when she rode up on horseback to grandma Knowles' farm at Tallula, Illinois, about twenty-five miles from Springfield. Papa was out in Colorado at the time, and we were living with her parents. Mama, not yet twenty years old, was teaching school in a nearby town, and would come home on weekends. I ran to her and she took me in her arms. That's about all I can remember that far back. But I later saw a few photographs of her around that time, and relatives commented years later that she had retained the fine complexion, lovely face, and wonderful, warm smile that she possessed back then. When I got old enough to notice such things, I saw that she also had rich brown hair and bright blue eyes, stood five feet-four and had a fine, well-developed figure.

Mama's father—my grandpa Richard J. Reynolds— was born on a tobacco plantation in Kentucky. Mama's mother, whose maiden name was Sarah Jane Watts, also was born on a Kentucky plantation. It was right next to the Reynolds' plantation. She and Richard knew each other from early childhood, and they fell in love when grandma was only fourteen and grandpa was several years older. The match was so strenuously opposed by both families that the young couple eloped and soon afterward moved to Indiana and later to Illinois. Grandma and grandpa never saw their parents again.

Grandma and Grandpa Reynolds had four children, including mama, Richard John, who was three years older than she, and two little girls, who died in infancy. Mama was born in Tallula, Illinois on October 4, 1856. She was christened Mary Elizabeth Reynolds.

When the Civil War came along, mama's papa enlisted and served with the Union Army. During the war he contracted consumption—later known as TB—and died a year after the war ended. Mama was then about eleven.

Grandma Reynolds was left almost penniless. Having a nice home, being a good cook, and very hospitable, she started serving meals to paying guests. My mama's brother, Richard began to work in a drugstore at the age of fourteen to help support our family. Mama was able to stay in school. Because she had a beautiful soprano voice, grandma and Richard managed to pay for voice lessons, too, for her. Later on, Richard became a partner in the drugstore and, eventually, the sole owner.

When mama was about thirteen, Grandma Reynolds married again, to an old-timer in Menard County by the name of William Knowles. He was a happy-go-lucky fellow who liked everyone and had many good friends. He took grandma and mama and Richard to his lovely farm, where he and grandma lived together happily for many years. But mama was soon to move far away.

Papa was born in 1847, and he grew up in Menard County. His father—my grandpa—John Summers, a Virginian by birth, had built up a farm in Menard County. He and his wife, whose maiden name was Frances Boles, had eight children, including papa, who was named John Colon Summers, after his father.

My grandpa Summers died quite early in life, during a terrible epidemic of typhoid fever, along with five of their children. Papa and his twin sister, Lydia Colon Summers, then two or three years old, were sent away to friends who kept them from catching the terrible disease. Years after that, my Grandma Summers married a farmer, Mr. Johnson. I never learned his first name because my grandma Fannie died three weeks after papa and mama were married.

When papa was a young boy he began drawing pencil sketches. He already knew in his boyhood that he wanted to be an artist. But in those days such talents as his were scoffed at. He met strong objections from all sides—especially from his stepfather Johnson, who was determined he should become a farmer. Papa told mama later how he often stole out to the big red barn and, safely hidden there, spent hours sketching the farm animals.

One Sunday in 1863, when he had not yet turned seventeen, he told his mother he was going down to the old swimming hole, along the Sangamon River. When he failed to return that afternoon, his mother and stepfather went looking for him. All they found were some of his underclothes. They assumed he had drowned, and for the next two years mourned for him.

Meantime, near the end of those two years of mourning, a tall young drum major for the Northern side became very ill from having had the contents of his knapsack—hardtack and soap, scrambled into one mess. Being starving hungry and with nothing else to eat, he partook of what he had. Hours later he became terribly sick. Believing he was going to die, he asked a fellow soldier to write to his dear mother. By now he deeply regretted having treated her so badly by running away and letting her think he had drowned. The letter was posted at the next village.

There was great rejoicing in the Johnson home and among their friends and neighbors who had known Johnny Summers. Grandma Fannie was even happier when she finally received a letter directly from her Johnnie. Stepfather Johnson decided then and there that he would never again cross the young man or discourage his desire to be an artist, if he would only return home. The young soldier returned home. A very happy reunion took place at the Johnson farm. They had a celebration that lasted a week.

His mother later told him, "I felt twenty years younger the day the postman handed me that letter and I learned my Johnnie was alive. God is good to me!"

Mama told me many times about first meeting papa when she was just turning fourteen and he was about twenty-two. Some mutual friends had introduced them at a party. So many times when I was growing up, mama would say to me, eyes sparkling at the recollection, "He was so tall and handsome, with his forelock of brown, curly hair and his big bright blue eyes. For both of us it was love at first sight!"

During their courtship he talked with her often about his dreams of becoming an artist or an actor or writer. But certainly he didn't want to be a farmer. They were married on April 1, 1872, in Petersburg, the County Seat of Menard County. I was born on January 14, 1873. Though I always wanted brothers and sisters, I was their only child.

When I was going on three, papa's health again took a turn for the worse. A doctor told him the climate in Colorado should be very good for him. So he left mama and me with Grandma and Grandpa Knowles in 1876 and went to Denver. Soon afterward he was offered a job working in a little store in Saguache, a high mountain valley in southwest Colorado.

He had to learn both Spanish and an Indian dialect, because many of the customers were of those backgrounds. He worked there until he got the ranch manager job at the Clayton Ranch and sent for mama and me. Now it was Spring, 1878, and we were part of a wagon train, just starting out from that Denver camping place and heading north to Cheyenne in Wyoming Territory.

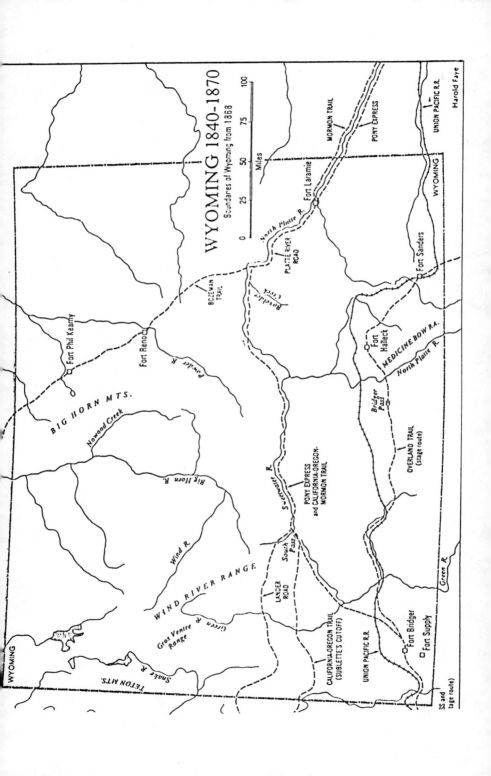

WYOMING 1840-1870

Boundaries of Wyoming from 1868

Miles

0   25   50   75   100

WYOMING

Harold Faye

UNION PACIFIC R.R.

MORMON TRAIL

PONY EXPRESS

Fort Laramie

North Platte R.

PLATTE RIVER ROAD

Horseshoe Creek

BOZEMAN TRAIL

Fort Sanders

Fort Reno

Fort Phil Kearny

Powder R.

BIG HORN MTS.

Nowood Creek

Big Horn R.

Wind R.

Fort Hallock

MEDICINE BOW R.R.

North Platte R.

Bridger Pass

Sweetwater R.

PONY EXPRESS and CALIFORNIA-OREGON-MORMON TRAIL

South Pass

OVERLAND TRAIL (stage route)

WIND RIVER RANGE

Gros Ventre Range

(Green R.)

Snake R.

TETON MTS.

WYOMING

LANDER ROAD

CALIFORNIA-OREGON TRAIL (SUBLETTE'S CUTOFF)

UNION PACIFIC R.R.

Fort Bridger

Fort Supply

Green R.

SS and stage route)

Chapter III

On the Trail to Oregon

The morning we left Denver for Cheyenne, where we'd finally begin heading westward for Oregon, everyone in our wagon train seemed in high spirits. There were now eight covered wagons in our party. They were made up of some of the people we had camped with on the outskirts of Denver. Papa said one man who knew the trail well to Laramie, was in the lead wagon.

Several wagons had a cow tied to the back end, walking along behind, just as we had our spare horse, Charlie, walking behind our wagon. Some had a few chickens in a coop built on the outside of their wagons. Another had a chair tied to the back, and a few wagons had wash tubs tied on the outside.

The evening before we left Denver, there was no campfire. Each family was busy repacking their wagon, including food and other supplies they had bought in town. They took as much dried food as they could, because that food would cost a lot more, if it was available at all, at trading posts along the way than it did in Denver. Because of these and other purchases, like coal oil and ammunition, some wagons were now overloaded. Only the most important things could stay. A couple of families in our wagon train sadly unloaded a piece or two of nice furniture like a buffet or a big mirror they had brought from the homes they had left.

All our covered wagons looked pretty much alike. I learned years later that most wagons were about ten to twelve feet long and around three and-a-half feet wide. They all had wooden sides two feet high or a little more. Papa usually sat on the left side, because he drove, and the big, iron footbrake was on that side. The wooden seat was so high that we looked down on the horses' backs. I sat in the middle, except when they let me get down and run along beside it, sometimes with other children, after we were on the trail.

In Denver papa had bought a mattress just the right size to fit snugly in the bottom of the wagon and leave room to squeeze past it on one side. It remained there the whole trip, except when we bought sacks of flour and rice and other dried food from some trading store along the way. Then those things went on the floor of the wagon, so we had to toss the mattress on top of them. Even then we usually managed to get it flat enough on top of the supplies so mama and I could lie down on it to rest as we traveled along. We especially appreciated it on hot, dusty days on the plains, when time seemed to drag. But no one thought of it then as a slow pace, since we had almost no experience with fast speeds as we did years later.

Some wagons were drawn by mules. While a couple of families with oxen were camped with us in Denver, they didn't travel with our wagon train. During our long journey west, we often saw oxen pulling wagons. Before we got to Oregon, I heard men say more than once that oxen's feet usually held up better than horses', and that oxen were better keepers. They could get along better than horses when grass was really scarce, which was often.

On the way to Cheyenne, about one week's travel north of Denver, the weather was mostly clear and the spring air pleasant but not really warm. Quite often we encountered showers. Sometimes the nights got cold and we found ice in the water buckets. On that part of the trip, we could look to the west and see far in the distance snow-capped foothills of the Rocky Mountains.

As we traveled from Denver to Cheyenne and Laramie, Laurie and I wanted to get together right away in camp and play. But we both had chores to do. As soon as we climbed down off the wagons, our mothers tied aprons on us, if we weren't already wearing them. We had to gather firewood. Later, on the plains, we had to gather dried cow chips. They made a fine, hot fire. So did dry sagebrush. Once in a while we found dried buffalo chips. But by 1878, there were only a few small herds of buffalo left.

After dinner, when we had helped dry dishes and sometimes do other chores, we were allowed to play until dark. Sometimes we played with our dolls or looked at the two or three picture books we had between us. Mostly, though, we liked to walk around camp and talk to other children and pet Laurie's family's horses and our three.

Once we left Colorado's valleys between forested hills, we began to come onto much flatter, rolling hills and range-land of northern Colorado and the southern part of Wyoming Territory. But there were always those mountains to the west.

An old bachelor in the party was bound for the Puget Sound country in Washington Territory. He and my parents became friends, and he talked with me quite a bit, too. One day he said. "Maudie, if you'll learn the names of all the main rivers we cross from here to Oregon, and tell me what they are when we get there, I'll buy you a nice book."

I told Mr. Hontune I'd like to try it. Children's books were scarce in wagon trains, and I wanted that book.

The first name I asked mama to enter for me on my list of rivers was the South Platte, part of which flowed through the outskirts of Denver. There followed some big creeks and small rivers, but they weren't marked and we didn't get their names.

I'll never forget one river crossing on the way to Cheyenne. That's when our own wagon almost got into big trouble for the first time. That particular day we were the last in line as we approached the river and the wagon train began to cross it one wagon at a time. While the others lined up and started crossing at a certain point, papa became impatient. He decided to cross a little farther down the river bank. He drove King and Sparkie only a short distance into the shallow part of the river when the horses began to get stuck. So did our wagon. We could feel it sink a little.

"Help! Quicksand!" papa shouted to the men in the first two wagons which by now already were safely across.

Seeing our danger instantly, they raced their wagons along the opposite bank to be nearer us. Then they turned so the backs of their wagons were in line with our horses. They tossed papa two big heavy ropes. They landed on King's and Sparkie's backs. Our horses already were very excited and the flying ropes frightened them more. Whinnying with terror, they tried to lunge in all directions. Papa talked calmly to them while he crawled out onto the wagon shaft which ran between them. Grabbing the ropes, he made them fast to the wagon's front axle. The men on shore fastened the ropes to the back axles of their wagons. Next, papa signalled to the men.

The six mules and horses from the three wagons fortunately managed to lunge forward at the same time. It was enough to free our horses and wagon from the quicksand's pull and get them safely ashore. Papa and mama looked badly shaken. They must have wondered what other unexpected dangers lay ahead. Soon the whole wagon train moved forward toward Cheyenne. Papa never again tried to cross at other than the chosen crossing site.

Mama and papa were excited when our wagon train crossed the border into Wyoming. One more day's easy travel brought us into Cheyenne.

(In 1878, Cheyenne was a small frontier town, only about ten years old. Still, the 1880 census shows it was the largest in Wyoming Territory, with a population of 3,456. Laramie was second largest, with a population of around 2,700 in 1880. After the eight wagon train families rested here for a day, topping up on provisions and filling barrels and buckets with fresh water, the wagons swung westward, heading for Laramie. Many people confuse Laramie with Fort Laramie, which is about ninety miles northeast of Laramie.)

The trip from Cheyenne to Laramie took only four days. Mama sometimes recalled years later how much greener the prairies between Cheyenne and Laramie looked than she had expected. She said the sagebrush was mostly still green and there were many patches of forest along the way. She said she thought those first days that this was the way it would be all across Wyoming. She was to find it getting dryer and dryer as we went past Laramie. Like Cheyenne, Laramie was ranching country, too.

After a brief stop in Laramie, we headed for Rawlins, traveling northwest for a few days and then westward. The country was even more wide open. The plains seemed to stretch endlessly ahead of us. It was now near the beginning of summer. The sun was hot and the trail was dusty. Even the wind, which seemed to blow quite a bit every day, was hot. Mama and I looked forward to the signal from the wagonmaster for the short noon stop—just long enough to give the animals a little rest and for us to eat a cold lunch the ladies had made the night before. We looked forward even more to the wagonmaster's signal late each afternoon that we were approaching our camping spot for the night.

We usually stopped when there were still a few hours of daylight left, so there was time to set up camp and do all the camp chores before dark. By contrast with the heat of the day, the nights continued to be quite cold. Papa told us as we were heading for Rawlins that from now on until we got to Oregon, we'd be traveling in sand and sagebrush, bleak hills and bare mountains.

Scattered here and there we saw beef cattle but hardly ever the ranch houses where the cows' owners lived. Most of the time we could still look far off in the distance, usually to the south, and see outlines of mountains. A blue haze—sometimes purplish—seemed to blanket them. At such times they looked soft and beautiful. Papa often gazed at the mountains. More than once he said he had a strong urge to stop and try to put a particularly pretty scene on paper.

Some days the prairie winds got so strong they nearly blew our wagons over. Once it did blow the canvas cover loose from one end of our wagon, even though papa thought he had tied it very securely.

Papa's health still wasn't very robust. It seemed like he still hadn't fully overcome whatever it was that damaged it during the Civil War. He had his up and down days. Sometimes when he felt poorly and we came to a little settlement, we would leave the wagon train and rest for a while. At such times mama would make him strong sage tea. He always said that her tea helped him feel better. Because of those stops, which began west of Laramie, it made things much lonesomer for mama and me. One morning I was to see Laurie's family pull out with the other wagons while we stayed behind. Waving to her, I wondered if we'd ever meet again. We never did. Yet we were continually meeting new people, also bound for Oregon. At times, we'd enjoy a few days or weeks traveling with them.

I learned on the wagon trains that most ladies addressed their husband, at least when others were present, as Mr. Olson or Mr. Travis. Not mama. Papa's dark brown, curly hair had been turning gray for some time. Now it was getting snow-white. Around this time, his twin sister, Lydia, wrote from Illinois that her hair also was getting very white. This convinced my parents it wasn't the climate or the alkali in the water which caused the fast change. It was, they decided, something he had inherited.

"Well, Johnnie Summers," mama said, "your white, wavy hair with your fresh, young complexion and the way you always stand straight as an arrow make you look young and distinguished." It was always "Johnnie" with her. I never heard her address him as Mr. except in some humorous situation.

Once in a while mama spoke longingly of the big meals we had enjoyed back in Illinois. Each time, papa reminded her of the fresh trout we'd had from the creeks and rivers in Colorado—fresher than from the best restaurants back in Illinois, he said. He also reminded her of the nice, fresh meat from deer, antelope, and sage hens. Still, mama and I sometimes got tired of wild game and longed for other kinds of food.

Mama said she longed for fresh potatoes, thick gravies, eggs, butter and milk, and she told papa so. She was a fine cook—mainly because he had taught her to cook after they were married. When she finished her wishing aloud about food, papa would then compliment her on how she made all the wild game taste the very best. And he'd find some way to make her laugh. After that, he might light his pipe, puff on it as if deep in his own thoughts. Then he'd draw her into dreaming aloud with him about our future in Oregon.

One hot day I suddenly saw a beautiful, shimmering lake, right up ahead of us on the dusty prairies. Near it were trees and green grass.

"Look! Look!" I shouted in great excitement, pointing to it.

Papa and mama turned instantly to where I pointed and gazed intently. They saw nothing. When I described what I was seeing and continued to point, papa said gently, "No, Maudie, that's not a lake. It's a mirage." I'd never heard the word. He explained to me that because of the particular mix of brilliant sunlight, prairie sand and condition of the air at the time, it just seemed like those things were out there. It was a very disappointing experience for me. I wasn't fully convinced until we ran right through what should have been the lake but was only more wagon tracks on the prairie. All three of us saw a mirage from time to time all the way to Oregon.

Riding for many hours, often over bone-jarring bumpy ground, made us all feel stiff and even sore. Sometimes papa turned the reins over to mama, and he got out and walked alongside or in front of the wagon for several hours. This was a common practice. We saw the men from other covered wagons doing the same. When papa got back on the wagon after walking, then mama and I might take our turn doing the same. We always felt refreshed afterward.

Traveling with a wagon train, we often saw men and boys riding horses. After hours in the saddle, they might swing down off their mounts and walk a while, leading the horses. They were working off stiffness, too. On one wagon train we saw a middle-aged lady ride quite often for a change from sitting in the family's wagon. Later on, when I was a little older, I was allowed to run by myself near the wagon, jumping sagebrush and greasewood like an antelope. I never got over my love of running, jumping and climbing.

During the two years papa had worked in Saguache, Colorado, first at the general store and later at the ranch, he and mama managed to save most of the money he earned. Before mama and I arrived at the ranch, he had used his hobby of studying minerals in his free time to go prospecting nearby. One day he found evidence of gold in samples of ore he brought in to get tested. He staked out a claim to the little mine. Later, he sold it to several other men for a fair price. He and mama saved that money, too. They said it was to help build up a ranch in Oregon.

Before leaving Saguache, mama took two long strips of lightweight white canvas and stitched them together to make a money belt for each of them. They put their twenty-dollar gold pieces in them and wore them around their waists next to the skin. This way there was no danger of losing the money. When they needed money on the trip, they'd open the belt inside the wagon and take out some coins.

During the covered wagons years, people often had to buy water when they traveled over the plains and came to a little settlement far from a river or creek. Sometimes it was a lone trading store. When we got to bigger rivers, there might be ferry fees. Sometimes we had to pay tolls: to some "nester" who charged "four bits"—a half-dollar—a wagon to drive through his homestead to ford a particularly easy and safe part of the river.

Chapter IV

Covered Wagon Ways

We had several real characters in our party at times. The one who stands out most strongly in my mind was "Old Susan"—a large, coarse woman. She probably wasn't past forty, but that was the nickname the wagon train people gave her. She had her own wagon and span of mules. Mama said she'd never before met or even seen anyone at all like her.

The lady could be humorous, I realized even as a small girl. And few people were more friendly or kind. She provided many laughs for the rest of the wagon train, usually by the ways she expressed herself. And she talked to those two mules like they were her wayward children. A good laugh was something very much needed and welcomed on the trail.

Hailing from Missouri, she had loaded her wagon with long leaf tobacco, for the purpose of swapping it to cover many of her expenses along the way. Places where other people had to pony up four-bits or even six-bits for water, or a ferry crossing, she would always turn to the man she owed money, looking perfectly innocent and helpless.

"Well, sar, mister, kin ye change my only twenty-dollar goldpiece?"

"No, I can't, lady," was the usual reply. Everyone in the wagon train knew what was coming next.

"Well, sar, I'm afeard the only thing I have to pay ye with is this 'ere good, long leaf tobaccer, an' I hate to part with it, fur I'll never see the likes o' it agin in this 'ere old wilderness country."

Of course, the ferryman or the rancher selling water immediately wanted the tobacco instead of money, so she always won out. More than once I heard papa laugh and say, "Old Susan can sit on her wagon seat while she's driving and spit tobacco juice in her mules' ears!"

Old Susan chewed tobacco all day long. It often looked to me like she really was trying to see how far and accurately she could spit it.

Riding that high seat day after day, we passed time partly by observing everything around us. One thing the three of us watched with amusement was the way King, the boss horse, who was a friendly big chestnut, always managed to stay on the best part of the well-worn wagon track. Some parts of the Overland Trail looked like two or three wagons could go along abreast. In other parts it was just wide enough for one wagon.

There were lots of rough stretches or spots. King always managed to end up on the best part of the trail. Sparkie, whose coloring was very similar to King's, but had a bigger white blaze on his face, often found himself on rougher ground. Time after time Sparkie would sidle over to King and half-lean against the wagon tongue, trying to nudge King out of the best part of the track, so he could walk in it.

But when even two or three horses are together, one always establishes himself or herself as boss horse. King clearly was boss. We all agreed, though, that he carried out his role in a gentlemanly way. When Sparkie challenged him, King usually lowered his ears and pretended he was going to bite Sparkie. He rarely did actually bite him. If his threat didn't work, then he'd throw his weight hard against the wagon tongue, toward Sparkie. Sparkie would quickly move to his own side, and the matter was ended for a while.

Charlie was our special pet. He was the friendliest. Maybe it was because he got lonely walking behind the wagon and getting all its dust. Papa would put Charlie in harness up in front and rested one of the other horses for a day or two if he showed any lameness or other leg or hoof problem. But he said Charlie didn't work as well up front as part of a team. Besides that, he was quite a bit smaller than the other two horses, so the harness had to be adjusted.

Every evening in camp, unless it was bad weather, I'd go over after chores and pet and talk with all three horses. Charlie always made a low, soft whinnying sound mama called "nickering." King and Sparkie whinnied noisily whenever they saw papa, mama or me coming toward them with some dried corn. If we gave a little treat to one, we had to do it for all three, because horses are like people in that respect. They like equal—or better—treatment. They can get jealous, like dogs or humans. They can show real happiness, and get upset or mad at other times.

Covered wagon people fed very little grain to their draft animals. There was no room to carry much of it, and it added weight for the draft animals to pull. Papa sometimes had a sack of dried corn in our wagon. He'd give a handful to the horses only when they had to work especially hard—like pulling up a steep grade or over rough trail. Mostly, though, they had to live on grass along the way. That was part of the reason most people tried to start in spring as soon as the grass was ripe enough for the draft animals to eat.

"Maudie loves horses so much," mama once said to papa as we drove along. "We should think about getting her a pony in Oregon."

"You bet she'll have a pony in Oregon!" papa said with spirit. Turning to me with a big smile, he said, "That's a promise!"

Mama and papa often sang favorite old songs to pass time on the trail—especially in good weather, and when things were going well, and when we were traveling alone. Traveling in a wagon train meant eating a lot of dust, especially if you were not very near the front of the line. They taught me the words to most of their songs and encouraged me to sing along with them. We sometimes heard people from other wagons singing, and we'd all sing around campfires at night.

We didn't have campfires often, though. Mama said people usually were too tired from the day's travel, getting supper, taking care of the stock, and doing other camp chores. Besides getting supper, mama made up a cold lunch for noons, and even a cold breakfast, if it was raining hard and it would be hard to start a cooking fire.

Both of my parents were good singers. Mama sang soprano and papa could sing either tenor or bass. Mostly they sang old favorite church hymns like *Bringing in the Sheaves, Rock of Ages*, and *What a Friend We Have in Jesus*. Among their old favorite songs were, *The Blue Danube, Silver Threads Among the Gold*, and *Mollie Darling*. Mama's first name was Mary, but her nickname was Mollie.

Looking back, I wonder how mama and the other ladies ever managed. Mama, like some other women, also did part of the driving. When we traveled alone or with only a few wagons, papa usually had to do his own shoeing. On the trail, horses' feet had to be trimmed and shoes reset or replaced every month or a little more, depending in part on how rough the ground was.

Life on the trail was as hard for women as for men. They had to do all the cooking over open fires, often burning their hands and heating their faces far beyond a comfort level. A small shift of wind might send smoke into their eyes, making them sting and water. Smoke clung to their hair and clothes. They washed the cooking utensils and dishes and helped their husbands haul water and gather fuel to burn— unless they had children old enough to take over some of those chores.

They rinsed a minimum of clothing almost daily; then when the wagon train stopped for a day's rest or longer, they did a full washing—if they were near a river or creek. There they usually washed them in cold water and home-made soap. Each family staked out a section of river bank to dry them in the sun. Often people on the trail had to wear pretty dirty clothes between washings, even though they had a change or two. The mother also had to mend all the clothes, unless there was another grown lady or big girl in the family to pitch in and help.

(When a man in a wagon train was too sick to drive, sometimes his wife was the only one to do so. Some women even used harness tools to try to repair the family's shoes. Beyond that, they took care of the children and acted as the family nurse, fixer of hurt feelings, and some tried to teach their children reading and writing on the trail. Of course, all covered wagon children old enough to be aware of the passing scene were getting a fine education in Western geography.)

(The men, beside doing most of the driving, tended to the feeding, harnessing and unharnessing, and they tried to find grazing for the stock. They repaired wagons and harness. In bigger wagon trains there might be at least one expert horseshoer. Men hunted for fresh meat and caught fish when they could.)

Despite the hardships, there were many relaxed, happy times. Mama said to me several times years later that our months on the trail were some of the happiest of her life. Looking back long after we got settled in Oregon, I wondered whether she would have felt the same if we had been like typical covered wagon families and traveled straight through in around six months.

It was about a week's travel by wagon train from Laramie to Rawlins. The train first headed generally north-west; then at around the half-way point it went westward. There was lots of sagebrush and scatterings of small pine groves on hillsides. But still the country is very dry, despite the occasional downpours of rain. The rain seems to disappear right into the sand. A little of it may flow for a short time into what were, hours or minutes earlier, dry creek beds.

(Less than two days before the wagons reached Rawlins, they had to cross a branch of the North Platte. This particular branch formed at the point where the Sweetwater and the North Platte Rivers met far to the north.)

(Like Cheyenne and Laramie, Rawlins was a tiny frontier community, created as a result of the building of the Union Pacific Railroad. By 1878, this little town looked, with its clapboard, mostly one-story buildings, like the setting for a tiny frontier town in a western movie. It had been in existence only about a decade and, in 1880, had a population of about 1,450.)

We stopped in Rawlins only long enough for families

to get more provisions, ask about trail conditions to Rock Springs and Green River, and to fill up with fresh water.

I listened to mama and papa dreaming together so many times, up on that wooden wagon seat, about the land they'd homestead and the ranch they'd build up out in Oregon. Mama, always the practical one, would say, "Johnnie, when we reach Oregon we must still have enough money left to set up the ranch and get sheep and hogs to raise." I heard her talk many times about how sheep multiply so fast, and how we could soon have a big flock. Papa was thinking more about a cattle ranch, I sensed. I know I was.

Mama was the one with the good business head, as she clearly demonstrated later. Papa was more of a dreamer, though he was intelligent, capable, and very honest. He also had a flair for numbers and bookkeeping. His disposition wasn't as sunny, so it didn't always carry him through tough situations the way mama's did for her. He was very temperamental. Sometimes he let his temper get the best of him. I wondered years later if mama—and his own mother—didn't spoil him too much.

During the travel westward from Rawlins, it was hot, windy and dusty most of the way. And there were lots of ups and downs in the trail. due to small hills and rolling land in some stretches. Rock outcroppings right in the trail were especially jarring and hard on the wagons. Small mountains and mesas—tablelands—looked very colorful. We continued to have strong winds quite often, and the farther we went, the drier and more light brown to tan the land looked.

When the wind came up strong, it made us feel even hotter. There had been one such day around noon on the open prairie, when the wind was extra strong. Blowing sand got into our eyes and throats. Even the horses tried to turn their heads away from it. After several hours of this, we suddenly came to a tiny ranch house with a sod roof, and several modest looking barns and sheds.

"Now that's pioneering!" papa said. "Maybe they'll be willing to put us up here 'til the storm's over."

He pulled off the trail, followed a rough track over to the sod shanty and climbed down, holding his hat so it wouldn't blow away. A care-worn looking young woman came to the door, holding a tiny girl. A small boy, maybe two years old, followed close behind, holding tight to her skirt. The lady welcomed us warmly, and invited us to come in and get out of the sandstorm.

Her husband, who looked quite a bit younger than papa, soon appeared from out back by the barn or shed, and helped get our horses into makeshift shelter behind the bigger shed. Inside the house it was sweltering. Despite the blowing sand, it was too hot to leave windows and doors completely shut. I felt nearly suffocated. A glance at mama showed me she felt the same. The lady went to the kitchen and came back with glasses of water. They had such a strong alkali taste, we could hardly drink them. Alkali water was known in those days as "gyp water." Maybe it was because people who drank its revolting taste felt gypped.

We accepted gladly the couple's invitation to have dinner with them and spend the night at the ranch. Mama brought in some dried food from our supply for part of the meals. We slept in our own wagon because the house was so small. During the night the wind died down.

On the trail again after breakfast, papa said he had saved enough water in our barrel for our horses. At least once a week on the whole trip he'd remind mama that we must keep the horses in good shape. If we lost them, we'd lose our wagon and all our possessions stowed in them. Surely mama was as aware of this as papa. We all used water very sparingly, except on joyful occasions when we came to a good clear creek, a small river or a little town.

Papa and mama got pretty excited about arriving at the Continental Divide. I didn't understand what that meant. Papa said it was the "backbone" of the country. From my later studies in school about the Continental Divide, and from talking with papa and mama about it while I was working on those lessons, I came to realize what they must have been trying to tell me when we crossed that Divide.

They maybe said something about the high Rockies ranges not being a solid wall of high mountains running solidly from the top to the bottom of our country, but that the high mountains drop way down here and there. Through those low places people can travel from one side of the Continental Divide to the other much easier than trying to go over one of the high mountains. The way mama and papa talked, it was clear they felt that this was a sign of making real progress in our travel to the West.

(At the point where Maudie and her family crossed the Continental Divide, the land is gently rolling—virtually desert in some places. It is a gap in the Divide, just as the famous South Pass on the Oregon Trail is a low point.)

Not long after crossing the Continental Divide, we came to a little place called Table Rock, because the main natural feature was a big rock shaped like a round table. It wasn't far off the trail. Sometimes the land was very badly broken up by what must have been creeks. They had worn deep gouges into the earth, twisting and turning in all directions. Now, being completely dry, they created barriers the wagons had to work around or through.

Chapter V

Heading For Green River Town

The effects of seldom having enough good drinking water and often not having enough grass for the horses probably had quite a bit to do with papa's starting to talk about our making a long stopover at Green River town, now only days away. He was having another of his fairly frequent bouts of "colic" around the time we crossed the Continental Divide.

Mama had asked if he wanted to stop and rest for a day or two. He said he wanted to keep going, since Green River was so close. I think Mama was as glad as I was to hear him say that. We did make a stopover, though, for a couple of days at Rock Springs, another small frontier town where, mama years later recalled several times, we got water that actually tasted good.

I could almost always find a few children around my age to play with in the evenings and on Sundays when we traveled with a wagon train. Now, with Green River only about two days west of Rock Springs, mama and I began to daydream about what we'd do during our long stopover. We'd get a good rest from the bumpy, swaying wagon ride and living in such cramped space. We'd be by a nice, clean, cool river. We could drink all the good-tasting water we wanted any time we felt like it. There would be shade trees, too—something pretty scarce back then in southwest Wyoming except in little towns. Maybe we'd even have some of those kinds of food mama told papa she longed for. I looked forward to such foods, too. But mainly I wanted playmates I'd be with for a while.

Our way of travel was different in two main respects from most other pioneer families headed westward in covered wagons. More than half the time we traveled alone. Some wagon train families tried to travel seven days a week. They did so for several reasons: to make supplies stretch, to keep ahead of wagon trains behind them and thus have more grass than they might otherwise have for their own livestock. And they wanted to be certain to arrive in Utah, Oregon or California before the snows began to fly.

(Some wagon trains stopped regularly on Sundays to rest. Surprisingly, many of those who did so, often reached their destinations before the wagon trains that went straight through. And the physical condition of the people who rested, and their livestock, often was better.)

We'd stop from time to time to rest at larger settlements, because of papa's health, to keep the horses in good shape, and to help cover expenses on the trip. Papa then would try to find temporary work. Their plan seemed pretty sound. Except for his colic, we still were in good health. King, Sparkie and Charlie looked much thinner than when we started, but they were still healthy enough to pull our wagon. And mama and papa had hardly touched the gold coins they started out with from Saguache.

We sometimes came across the remains of a cow, horse, mule, or ox that had died along the way. Near these sad remains we once saw an abandoned wagon. Parts were missing. Papa said either the owners or people they were traveling with might have taken them, or other people following behind them who needed a spare wheel, axle or other part. Mama would gaze intently at them, like she was going to cry.

As we got closer to Green River town, our excitement grew. Papa said we'd probably stay there until next spring. By now summer was about over. The little town, came into view. Even from a distance, Mama looked very pleased with it. She said the place looked like it was going to live up to her hopes for it.

But Green River also came close to being the end of the journey for our little family.

Chapter VI

Long Stopover in Green River Town

King, Sparkie and Charlie seemed to share our excitement as we approached the edge of Green River town. Did they sense our moods? Horses, I learned as I grew older, are very good at that. Or had they learned that when we came to a town we often stopped for a few days? That meant a good rest for them, and sometimes better forage. Or did the horses simply see all that clean river water and think, as we did, that at last they could drink their fill of good water?

The little community looked lively and friendly. It had trees and some yards had grass. I saw a church, too. Several people smiled at us as we drove up the main street, and two girls who looked to be around my age, waved to us. Mama and I waved back. Papa picked out an open field a little beyond the edge of town, close to the river, for our camping place. We saw wagon tracks and campfire circles—signs that this might be a regular stopping place for covered wagons traveling through here on the way westward.

While papa took care of the horses, and mama began to unpack supper things, I put on my "chores apron" and began to look for dead twigs and dried cow or oxen chips to burn in our cooking fire. Papa took a big tin water bucket in each hand to the river and came back with water that was clear and cold. Soon mama had a hot meal ready. I was very excited about spending the winter in this nice little town, living in a real house again for a while, and making friends with some girls and boys my age. After evening chores, we all turned in early and had a good night's sleep by the cool river.

During breakfast papa sat back, relaxed, and sipped his coffee. He said he was going out that morning to find us a house to rent, and he'd try to get a job for the winter. Within a few days he had a job working at the town's livery stable, and he found us a cozy little house to spend the winter in. It turned out to be very pleasant and comfortable.

One of my many happy memories of our stay in Green River was of papa's giving me horseback riding lessons. Even though I was now nearly six, he was very cautious about it. He insisted on leading the horse. Maybe if it had been a small, gentle pony, he would have let me ride all by myself. The horse he had selected for me belonged, as I recall, to one of his friends and was kept there at the livery stables. It seemed very tall to me, and friendly enough but lively. Those lessons, along with my strong friendship with King, Sparkie and Charlie, made me all the more eager to have a pony of my own when we got to Oregon.

Our little family had a near-tragedy one cold winter morning. My parents took me down to the river, which was frozen over. It was about two blocks from where we lived. Close to the river bank the ice was very thick. Papa decided it looked strong enough all the way across. He walked safely to the opposite side. Then he began to walk along the far shore, looking for and shooting ducks. Mama and I remained on the town side of the river, watching him.

After a while, papa had shot several ducks, which fell onto the ice in different places. As he began looking for a fourth duck, he called to mama to come out and pick up the ones he had shot.

Before starting across, mama turned to me. "Don't come onto the ice!" she ordered firmly.

She walked along our side of the river's edge until she was about opposite where the first duck fell; then she started across. I began to follow her, not wanting to be left alone. About the time she reached the center of the frozen river, I heard the horrifying sound of cracking ice. Suddenly it broke. Down mama went. She began to sink into the flowing river. As she was going under, she half-turned, saw me, and shouted, "Go back!"

I stood there in shock, frozen with fear and horror. I stared at the point where she went down, and at the same instant I began crying and screaming wildly to papa. He soon saw what had happened, and began making his way rapidly toward her. By now mama was out of sight under the ice, except for one little hand grasping the broken edge. Then I saw one of her arms come up out of the icy water. She groped and managed to get her elbow flat on top of the ice, where it had broken. In a few seconds more, she had her other elbow and then both shoulders out of the water.

When I had seen her go under, I was simply terrified. "Oh, mama, mama, mama..." I kept moaning and sobbing, half to myself, "...please, please come back!"

In a few more seconds papa was beside her, lying flat on the ice. He grabbed for and caught both of her wrists.

Very slowly he pulled her body upward. The ice cracked again. I thought I was going to die of fright. Then, somehow, he had her out of the water and was pulling her toward shore. A few seconds more and they were on solid ice. Papa took her nearly frozen body in his arms and held her close, all the time talking to her.

I could hear mama's strong sobbing and the faint sound of his voice as he tried to comfort and reassure her. He carried her as fast as he could by a safe crossing place to the town side of the river, to which I had retreated. I followed them, still sobbing and frightened. As he carried her up from the river bank and onto the street, people stopped and looked curiously. Papa gave no explanation but kept walking as fast as he could with her. Every minute or so from the time he crossed the ice with her, he would murmur, only half-aloud, "Thank God! Thank God!"

Finally, walking along the street where we lived, a neighbor lady whom mama knew stepped onto the street ready to go somewhere. She turned, saw us coming, and realized immediately that something awful had happened. She spoke briefly to papa, then rushed ahead to our house, opened the front door and went right over to pull back the blankets on the bed. They got her dried off, into a nightgown and into bed.

Meantime, the neighbor lady had found time to stoke up the wood-burning kitchen range and put water on for tea. While papa fed mama the tea, the neighbor lady rushed back to her own house and returned soon with more heavy woolen blankets. She later alerted some of mama's and papa's other friends and neighbors, who brought in hot dishes. Then, probably sensing that papa and I wanted to be left alone with mama, they departed.

That evening when mama began to feel a little stronger,

she started talking. Up until then she hadn't spoken a word that I heard. Though I can to this day still vividly recall the incident, I can remember only the sense of mama's own words. Half-crying, she spoke in a small voice, only two or three words at a time. She kept repeating them after a few minutes of silence. "I'm alive! Thank you, God!" and "Oh, Johnnie! Maudie! I'm so glad to be alive!" At one point she told us, "I thought I was gone. I kept telling myself if I never give up, I'll live. We did it! A miracle! God is good." A day or two later, when mama and I were alone, she told me we must show our gratitude by helping the poor, unfortunate people.

That night she looked up at papa and said in a little child's voice, "I'll be all right again soon, won't I?"

Mama was young and healthy. In a few days she was up and around again, seeming fully recovered. In the weeks that followed, she often recalled the near tragedy and the miracle that she was still alive. In our home, we never again spoke of ducks. I can't recall that papa ever hunted them again.

The remainder of our stay in Green River was happy and uneventful. For more than a year, mama had been teaching me the alphabet and numbers. During our stay, she made me sit down with her for about two hours almost every weekday, except in summer, and taught me enough so I could now form simple words and do some addition and subtraction. Papa worked the whole time at the livery stable. He always seemed happy working around horses.

Mail in those days was carried by stagecoaches along parts of the Overland Trail. They often were delayed, at least in southern Wyoming Territory, in winter by bad weather, including snow, and in early spring by rushing creeks caused by melting snow. And there were high winds which blinded drivers and horses. I heard someone say that blowing sand even cut the paint off the stagecoaches. Oldtimers in some of the windier places would say, "The wind was so strong it blew the feathers right off the chickens."

I recall mama telling our friends and grandma and grandpa years later about life in Green River. She said word somehow always got passed when the stagecoach was drawing near. It was a form of diversion for some of the town people, young and old, including mama and me, to gather in front of the general store. It also served as the post office. We watched the stage arrive, saw passengers it carried, and waited for the mail to be sorted. Meantime, people all visited with each other. When the stagecoach drew up and stopped in front of the waiting people, I can still recall that the horses, usually four of them, were all sweaty and breathing hard. Sometimes sweat foam looked like whipped cream under parts of the harnesses

It was hard for people to get their mail while they were traveling along the Overland Trail. Mama would, like other wagon train people, send the names of little towns we expected to reach by a certain time. Often, though, there were problems getting the mail through. And sometimes we didn't stick to the travel schedule we had given. Thus, too many times we, and other people, didn't get any mail. That was always a great disappointment, especially for mama. It was much easier when we knew we were going to stop over in a town for some time, like we did in Green River. But most covered wagon trains didn't travel like we did; they kept going.

At Green River, mama got mail from Grandma and Grandpa Knowles almost every time the stage came in. Mama often sounded homesick for them. When she didn't receive a letter after the stage arrived, she was a little blue for a day or two. Some of grandma's letters contained money. Mama told me several times when she received those checks that she'd save them so the three of us could make a visit back to see her family and papa's in Illinois.

Early in the spring of 1880, papa grew restless and wanted us to start again for Oregon. By now we had been in Green River for nearly eighteen months. Looking back, I am surprised that they didn't feel more of a sense of urgency to get out to the Oregon country as quickly as possible in order to get a good choice of remaining homestead land. I had turned seven that January. Hearing them talk together, I knew both felt good about the amount of money they had been able to save and add to their belt pouches of twenty-dollar gold pieces.

So one spring morning we were on our way again. King, Sparkie, and Charlie acted as eager as we to hit the trail West once more. From talk between mama and papa about Salt Lake City and the Great Salt Lake, I looked forward to seeing them, maybe even with more excitement than I had about coming to Green River.

I'd have been excited, too, had I known as we moved twelve to fifteen miles closer to Salt Lake City each day, about the new adventure for mama and me that lay ahead, beginning in only a few more weeks.

Chapter VII

On to Utah Territory

We got started each morning while it was still cool—sometimes before the sun even came up. At first, a sweater felt good. The early morning sun warming our necks and faces also felt good. That was always surprising to me, since a few hours later the sun usually was uncomfortably hot. And we found the wind very strong in that southwest corner of Wyoming, as we neared the Utah border.

Horses don't like wind. Papa said he thought it is due to some instinct that warns them of danger from falling tree branches and trees blown down. Just as blowing sand stung our faces and got in our eyes, it was irritating to the horses. When we stopped for mid-day meals and to rest the horses, we seemed always to be looking for shade or shelter from the wind. Both were hard to find on the desert. While the days could get real hot, the nights were cool—sometimes cold, so we slept well. We felt sorry for the horses, who weren't getting enough grass or water.

Sometimes, traveling alone, we followed a few days behind a wagon train. Papa found it necessary at such times to graze our horses a quarter mile or more off the trail in order to find grass. When I'd wish aloud that we were with the other wagons, which I often did, papa would remind me that we were avoiding all that dust, and things weren't so crowded and unsanitary. What he didn't add was that he was pretty much a loner by nature.

What made a good campsite, besides the grass, papa told mama and me many times, was a place flat enough for the wagons, drinking water nearby, and something to burn in the cooking fire: dry sagebrush or dried oxen chips. We seldom got close to any trees, so we couldn't often look for limbs or twigs. Papa also liked to camp in a place where we could add antelope, sage hens, or other wildlife to our always limited food supply. Occasionaly, a few fish from a creek or river were a big help.

(Buffalos were rarely seen in 1880 because they had been hunted and slaughtered almost to extinction. Following the earliest explorers to the West were hunters and trappers, traders and other fortune seekers. Large numbers of buffalos had been recklessly—even wantonly—killed off by hunters interested only in their hides and tongues. Indian tribes had hunted them much more responsibly: taking only enough for part of their food supply.)

(Heaviest wagon train travel West over the Oregon Trail and other well-known trails such as the Overland Trail, had taken place during the 1840's through the 1860's. During that period more than 350,000 men, women and children came by prairie schooners, buggies, on horseback, and some on foot. Historian John Unruh, in his fine book, *The Plains Across*, reported that between 1840-1859, more than 50,000 people traveled to Oregon and more than 230,000 to Utah and California. Merrill J. Mattes estimated in his *The Great Platte River Road* that about 350,000 people traveled westward on the trails between 1841-1866. Historian T. A. Larson and others have noted that covered wagon travel West continued through the 1870's, and there was a small amount in the 1880's and beyond.)

(These pioneers took their toll, too, on the remaining buffalo herds. At least a small number of early covered wagon people, evidence shows, hunted for sport rather than taking just enough for meat along the way.)

About a week after leaving Green River, we came to Wyoming Territory's western border and crossed into Utah Territory. The land as far ahead as we could see was desert and rolling prairie land. Later, we began to see snow-capped mountains far ahead. Papa said we should reach Salt Lake City in about a week. His estimate turned out to be a good one. During our time in Green River, papa talked with several men who had been in Salt Lake City, so my parents had some idea of what to expect. What they knew must have been good. They grew more excited the closer we got to the big Mormon settlement out on the desert, with its great salt lake and nearly surrounded by mountains.

A few days out from Salt Lake City, our spirits brightened even more when we began to follow or go past clear flowing creeks or small rivers. Now the snow-covered peaks of the magnificent Wasatch Range and other mountains that nearly surround the city looked much bigger.

As we got nearer, mama told papa how much she'd like to see Grandma and Grandpa Knowles again. Papa knew she wanted to take those checks her mother and step-father were sending her, and have all three of us go back some day to Illinois on a visit.

"Mollie," he said, turning to her with a big grin, "I've

been thinking quite a bit lately about you and your mother and stepfather. It'd be easier if you and Maudie make the trip back to Illinois from somewhere along the way—where the Union Pacific has a station. That way it'll be a shorter trip and cost much less than if we wait until we get to Oregon. There's a Union Pacific stop in Ogden. It's only a couple days' travel north from Salt Lake City. You and Maudie could take the train from there right to Illinois."

"Oh, Johnnie!" mama cried out with great emotion. Tears flowed down her cheeks, and she smiled very happily at the same time. "That would be so wonderful! The three of us will go together."

Papa beamed at her happy reaction. "No, Mollie," he said. "I couldn't stand any more of those hot Illinois nights in summer. While you and Maudie are visiting, I'll get a job in Ogden and I'll take care of the horses."

So it was settled. One day we rolled into the outskirts of Salt Lake city almost at sunset. There were nice dirt roads in the city. I was surprised to see how big the place was. I guess I was expecting something a bit bigger than Green River. There were many nice one and two-story homes, usually behind fences. I recall, too, that nearly every yard seemed to have trees.

The famous Mormon Tabernacle, which later became so well-known around America, was already built. I was amazed to find out here on the frontier this beautiful, long building with its roof rounded on both sides and on both ends. The roof was supported by pillars all around it. A few hundred yards away, mama, papa, and I marveled at a strikingly beautiful building under construction, with two stories already finished. This was to become the Mormon Temple. Already, nearby, there was completed and in use another nice big church with a tall steeple.

Everyone mama and papa talked with along the streets seemed friendly. One man guided us to a campground used by wagon trains. It was on the outskirts in a green, quiet place surrounded by trees. There we remained for about two weeks. My only disappointment—and I thought my parents shared the feeling—was that the great Salt Lake we'd been looking forward so much to seeing and at least wading in, wasn't in sight. Papa explained that it was some distance from town, but we'd get over to see it soon. When we did get there a day or two later, it lived up fully to the mental pictures we had built up about it. After many months in the desert-like Wyoming country—except for Green River, it seemed so wonderfully refreshing to be around all that beautiful, clean looking water. Salt Lake City impressed me as a huge place in 1880.

(Actually, the city had a population then of about 32,000. It was bigger than any other community between there and the West Coast, and was about the size of Denver. The whole Territory's population in 1880 was 144,000. More than 100,000 had arrived after 1870.)

(Not all Mormons came by covered wagon or on horseback. A large number of poor immigrants from Europe and some poor Americans from the Midwest came on foot, pulling two-wheeled carts piled high with whatever possessions they had and could load on them. Pulling those carts must have been terribly hard, much of the time in the searing heat of the desert, and with shelter from storms only if they carried and put up a tent. On the other hand, they didn't have to worry about feeding and watering livestock and keeping their hoofs and bodies in good shape. They didn't have to try to get covered wagons over rough spots, up and down steep hills and bluffs. Fording shallow rivers was probably easier with handcarts.)

While we were in the campground, people from the city came by and introduced themselves. Some men and women even dropped by once in a while in the days that followed and visited with us. They told us what a nice place Salt Lake City was to settle down in. Some encouraged us to think about it.

When we prepared to leave for Ogden, so mama and I could catch the train to grandma's, some of the friends we had made came to see us off. After our farewells, papa lifted the reins and called to King and Sparkie to move out. They suddenly jerked forward. I was kneeling on the bed in the rear of the wagon, leaning out the oblong hole made by rolling the canvas at that end part way back. When the horses lunged, I tumbled out of the wagon, hitting my head on the ground. Papa and mama didn't know I'd fallen out. The wagon kept going.

"Hey, stop! Whoa! Wait!" different male voices began shouting excitedly to papa, while running as fast as they could to get alongside the driver's seat. Finally, papa saw and heard them and stopped.

"You lost your little girl!" one man shouted.

Two ladies dusted me off and felt my arms, legs and head to make sure I was all right. Nothing was damaged but my pride, and my dress was a little dirty. Papa made me promise I would never lean out of the wagon again. They reminded me of the story still circulating through wagon trains then that years earlier a little six-year old boy fell out of a wagon and was run over by its wheels and killed. I never leaned out again.

Ogden, not very far north, took only a few days to reach. On the way, mama told papa how impressed she was with Salt Lake City. We'd already made a couple of visits to the great, shimmering lake. "I believe we'd like it here,

Johnnie," she said. "Just think of that marvelous lake. Wouldn't it be healthful and fine to live near it?"

Papa turned to mama, looking quite surprised and not at all pleased the first time she brought up the subject.

"Do you suppose Oregon has anything so fine?" she asked him, not slowed down by his negative reaction. "I can see opportunities here. Can't you?" Mama kept talking. When she finished, papa, still looking flushed and irritated, answered.

"Mollie, Oregon must be the finest place of all, from what I hear. If it isn't what it's cracked up to be, I'll be muchly disappointed. If we thought of going anyplace other than Oregon, we might try California. I might find a gold mine. But I think we'd better go on to Oregon. There must be more opportunities there, like so many people say. Let's go see for ourselves."

Ogden was what people called a "jerkwater town" back in those days. It had few people. Papa quickly found a job helping in a general store. One day shortly after that, he put us both on the train—a direct line to St. Louis and Kansas City.

(Ogden's population in 1880 was about 6,000. But it was on the Union Pacific line. The railroad provided an important link with big cities and to their markets. It also created many local jobs.)

The trip to Illinois was uneventful, except for my getting a cinder embedded in my eye when I stuck my head out the window to see better. Mama had warned me not to lean out like that. It took a doctor to remove the cinder.

There were no sleepers or reclining chairs on the train. We had to sit up all the way. There were no diners, either. Most people carried picnic baskets filled with food. At one end of the coach car was a big, round iron stove, on top of which passengers could make coffee or tea. There also were "butcher boys." At mealtimes one would come walking down the aisle selling food. He would carry it in a big, shallow box held in front of him by a heavy leather strap which went around his shoulders. Mama bought some canned salmon. It was the first time I ever tasted it. I thought it was some of the best food I'd ever eaten.

We had a delightful reunion back at Grandma and Grandpa Knowles' big farm outside of Petersburg, Illinois. Then we spent nearly three happy, relaxing months being spoiled and pampered by grandma and grandpa, and visiting with many relatives. When our time was up, we returned by Union Pacific to Ogden. Papa was waiting for us on the station platform, looking as excited as mama and I felt. It was such a warm, happy reunion. We had missed him so much and it was plain that he had missed us greatly.

"We'll head for Oregon country after you and Maudie are well-rested," papa said. Mama said she was ready and eager to get back on the trail. I certainly was. A week after our return, we left Ogden and headed north toward Idaho Territory. Mama said she had read it was a land of tall mountains and great forests. We'd heard about very serious Indian attacks in eastern Idaho Territory in years past. People in Ogden had assured papa, though, that now the Indians were not at all likely to attack us. Still, we held our breath.

Chapter VIII

We Reach the Oregon Border

At Ogden, mama and papa had become acquainted with several other covered wagon families headed for Oregon. They all seemed to like the looks of each other, and agreed to travel together. They turned out to be fine people—as most wagon train people we had traveled with were—and some became lasting family friends.

Leaving Ogden, we headed northward for the Idaho Territory border, about seventy-five miles away. The first few days we were in a wide valley. We seemed close to the towering Wasatch Range on our right. On the way to Ogden, people in our wagon train often had to pay Mormon ferry men to take us across small rivers and streams. After paying maybe five different times, papa said, sounding peevish, "We're leaving too much money here on the rivers!" Actually, he had paid river ferry men a number of times, beginning around Laramie.

All three of us were refreshed and rested from months

off the trail. Our horses seemed the same. So we were all in fine spirits. We sang a lot that first week out. Mama and papa spent hours every day exchanging stories about their experiences during the three months we were apart. Mama told about visiting with her brother, Richard Reynolds, the druggist, and with papa's twin sister, Lydia, and her daughter—my cousin Mollie. She gave him the latest news about all their old friends back in Menard County. And she described in detail some of the wonderful dinners Grandma Knowles had prepared for us.

Listening to the part about the sumptuous food, papa said, "This all whets my appetite for my favorite supper. Let's have it tonight!" We did. His favorite supper—almost any time—was hot baking powder biscuits covered with gravy, baked beans, pan-fried trout browned to perfection, as he had painstakingly taught mama to cook them, and a cup of coffee. Since he knew there were no nice trout to be caught right around there, he had to settle for salted bacon as a substitute.

During the first week out of Ogden, the horses were lively as crickets. Papa had a way of talking about them at such times. "They're really on the bit!" he'd say. He meant they were paying full attention and pulling with the bits in the back of their mouths, and not dawdling along, with bits hanging loose. I thought they felt extra spirited partly because they were now with other horses in the wagon train. Another way horses are like humans is that they like company. Most likely it's the ancient herd instinct.

Papa and mama both noticed that our horses were in better shape than many other wagon train horses. Papa said it was because we stopped often to rest and hunt and sometimes for him to work. They were still saving all they could to set up that Oregon ranch.

Most of the way to the Idaho Territory border, the land alternated between flat to rolling, dry plains and hills. At a couple of places we crossed the Bear River in northern Utah. Our trail twisted and turned quite a bit as we moved farther northward, near the border. Most of the way it was still mostly sand and sagebrush, but the nights were still cold, so we slept fine.

It all sounded so familiar again to hear coyotes howling off in the distance at night. It didn't bother us one whit. They were different from the wolves, which sneaked right up into the camps of some wagon travelers we had talked with back in Wyoming Territory. Wolves tried to take any food they could grab and run with. Somehow, we managed to avoid close contacts with wolves. We only saw coyotes in the distance.

I was disappointed when our wagon train reached the Idaho Territory border. I couldn't see any borderline. Papa said a small pile of rocks near the trail marked the border. This was a very happy event for my parents. "Oh, Johnnie! Oh, Maudie!" mama said with great feeling, "isn't this wonderful? All we have to do now is travel across Idaho and we'll be in Oregon!"

Traveling northward in Idaho, we'd occasionally see a lone ranch. While waiting for our wagon's turn at river crossings, we'd often stop and talk with people and water the horses. From the time we began our covered wagon travels, I was very conscious of the importance of our keeping our water barrel at least partly filled if we possibly could. A barrel full of water is very heavy, so it was a problem for papa to decide how much to carry. Often, out on the desert we were away from any water source. Could he depend on creeks and rivers up ahead not to be too muddy or have too much alkali—or to be running at all? He didn't want more hard work for King and Sparkie.

On sandy trails week after week the wooden wheels would dry and shrink. This made extra work for papa, and for every other wagon. The men soaked them in rivers and creeks as much and often as they could, but it never seemed enough. The way we traveled—stopping so often—papa managed to keep our wheels in good enough shape so he never lost one.

After doing all his other camp chores, he sometimes had to take off the wheels one at a time and spread a heavy, dark grease on the axles. I watched with fascination as papa dipped his fingers into the bucket of grease, then rubbed it onto each axle. It looked like fun. I asked him to let me help do it. He said no, I'd get all dirty.

For amusement on the desert, I'd sometimes try to count prairie dogs, as their heads bobbed up in a dozen places at the same time. Once papa shot at one, and they all disappeared immediately. We always had to keep our eyes peeled for rattlesnakes—especially around rocks.

Mama kept reminding me that if I wanted to win the book Mr. Hontune, the old bachelor, had promised me when he was with one of our wagon trains, I must write down and memorize every good-sized river we came to. When we reached the Bear River, it looked pretty muddy in places. I said I didn't want to write it in. Mama pointed out that it was a good-sized river, and I should include it. By now, my list filled several pages.

Breaking camp in the cold dawn after our first night in Idaho, we continued northward. Most days we stopped at noontime for an hour or two to rest the animals and to have a small lunch. This part of Idaho was unexciting to me. Here were more sand and sagebrush, and low hills here and there. We had been spoiled by the beauty of the mountains and water around Salt Lake City.

One day, about halfway from the Idaho border to Fort Hall, our wagon train came to a place where another road took off from it to our left. Someone had put up a crude sign on a post. It pointed to the west. The one word, which looked like someone had burned it into the wood with a hot poker, read: CALIFORNIA.

(Oregon Trail researcher-writer Irene D. Paden described vividly in her book, *Wake of the Prairie Schooner*, first published by The MacMillan Company in 1943, how this cutoff trail to California was first tried in 1849, during the gold rush. Starting six miles west of Soda Springs and bearing generally west and southwest to the Raft River area, it was known as Hudspeth's Cutoff—or Myers Cutoff—for the two men who first led a wagon train across it. From there, wagon trains went on to the Humboldt River in Nevada, then on into California. Follow-on covered wagon trains bound for California used it as a shortcut compared with the usual route. The latter ran northwestward to the Snake River, followed the Snake southwestward, then cut south by the Raft River area. Both trails eventually merged.)

One late afternoon we came to a destination we had heard so much talk about: the Snake River. There we made camp near the river's bank. While my first look at the Bear River had not pleased me, I liked the Snake River at once. It looked cleaner and more refreshing. We were told that Fort Hall once stood nearby and was a big help to covered wagon people because they could buy badly needed provisions there. But the Fort was long gone.

(Fort Hall was built as a trading post on the Snake River in 1834 by an adventurous young New England trader, Nathaniel Wyeth. It was taken over after two years and operated for nearly twenty years by the Hudson's Bay Company, when they abandoned it. Spring floods later washed away part of what remained.)

(Irene Paden, described in her book cited above, how a medical doctor, Minnie Howard, whom she and her husband met in Pocatello, Idaho, and whose hobby was researching local history, led them one summer day in 1935 to the remains of old Fort Hall. Dr. Howard also located for them the monument Oregon Trail pioneer Ezra Meeker had placed at the original site of Fort Hall in 1916. Dr. Howard had been with Mr. Meeker when he placed the monument. They found the ruins of old Fort Hall and the monument not under water, as the Padens had been told earlier by others, but "...hidden under a four-foot growth of wheat grass....")

(The original Fort Hall was located close to the Snake River and about eight miles from the present day village of Fort Hall, which is now part of the Fort Hall Indian Reservation for the Shoshone and Bannock Tribes.)

When we came to beautiful scenery, we'd often admire it together. Then sometimes papa would tell me again how some day when we got settled, he and I would paint many of those scenes from memory. Whenever I drew a picture on my school slate, he showed interest in it. Sometimes he suggested changes to make it look better. He always encouraged me to keep drawing.

Now our wagon train headed for Boise, around 300 miles to the west. We followed the great Snake River. It was called that because of the way it wiggled and wound around so much. A boy in our wagon train told me it empties into a big river we'd come to one day. It was called the Columbia.

We were still in sand and sagebrush, with a scattering of impressive looking mesas. The livestock were now more often getting better water to drink.

Indians in this part of the country rode horses which were small, spotted, and might have two or three colors. The Indians, and some of the white settlers, referred to them as pinto cayuses. I was fascinated to see some had eyes that looked white and glassy. Stockmen and cowboys had started years before we got out West to buy them for herding cattle. The horses had a reputation for being smart and swift, with special ability to follow, at high speeds, every twist and turn of a cow their rider was pursuing. We later heard stories from cowboys about how some of those ponies had been known, when mad, to bite. One rancher told papa there were a few cases in which a pony, when angered, even struck out with his front hoof at a man.

About two weeks out from Fort Hall to Boise, the wagons came to a placed called Rock Creek. It flowed into the Snake. We stopped at a good camping place. But between Fort Hall and Boise, I recall the country being mostly dry and often rocky. Often it seemed like endless sagebrush and sand. I thought, from papa's and mama's earlier talk, we'd see more trees than we did.

I had entered the names of several more rivers. Of these, the Clearwater, about three-quarters of the way, was my favorite. In that dry country, it looked so pure and sparkled in the sunlight. I remember also seeing in that area several waterfalls made by drops in the river bottom. Once in a while we came to nice bunch grass. The wagon train men would hobble the animals and let them graze on it until bedtime. Then they usually brought them in and tied them to the wagons. Many times I have heard men talking and agreeing it is surprising how far a horse with hobbles can travel from the camp in a night.

We were all excited to pull into Boise—known earlier as Fort Boise. It was a very pleasant little town. We felt we were back again in civilization. The first day there, papa and mama looked up Mr. and Mrs. Goff, whom they had known in Colorado. The Goffs invited us to dinner. The meal she served that night was a grand change for us. Since leaving Fort Hall, we'd had a heavy diet of jackrabbits, sage hens and quail, along with some nice fish once in a while.

During dinner, both the Goffs talked enthusiastically about Boise. They said it was a promising place.

(Fort Boise started as a fur trading station back in 1834, and was originally located along the Oregon Trail, near the river and some distance west of the present townsite.)

Because mama and papa wanted to stay over a few days in Boise, we left the wagon train. When we started out again, I caught their excitement over being so close to the Oregon border. We'd cross into the promised land in a few days! Now, day after day, we moved up the Snake River valley toward where we'd cross into Oregon.

We began to see more and more little farms, but they were still pretty widely scattered. Their barns always were bigger than the thrifty looking houses. As I recall, the farms all had fruit trees. Most farms had rows of poplar trees for shade and wind buffers. We began to see more herds of beef cattle and sheep, and sometimes quite a number of hogs and chickens. In more and more places we also saw forests of pine and fir.

Now, within hours of reaching the river crossing point excitement ran high. We'd be ferried over. Then we'd step onto Oregon soil. The promised land! Soon the ferry landing came into sight. So did our view of Oregon on the far side of the river.

I looked up and gazed inland for a long time. What I saw was spirit shattering to me. More dry, dusty prairie land. Bare brown mountains in the distance. My excitement, which had built to a peak in the preceding days, now collapsed.

I was an imaginative, nearly eight year-old girl by now. I had come to picture lush, green valleys, lovely lakes, rich farms, fruit trees bending down with apples and pears and peaches.

I felt a sense of betrayal. Oregon didn't look nearly as good to me as many places we had left behind: Boise, Salt Lake City, Green River, Denver. I looked up, ready to cry, and studied mama's and papa's faces. To my great surprise, papa was grinning broadly. But he didn't say a word. I thought he must be waiting for mama's reaction. Her expression told me plainly that her introduction to Oregon was like mine. Papa lifted me into his arms and wiped my tears with the back of his hand. He listened to why I was hurting, then explained that many parts of Oregon are indeed lush and green like I'd pictured. It was the eastern part of Oregon that was dry.

The barge that ferried us across was a big one, with ropes and a rudder on the end of a long pole to help guide us in the strong current. The ferrymen were very nice and quickly helped us load the horses and wagons. They seemed to sense mama's and my disappointment. They said when we looked around the Oregon country we'd be sure to like it. We made the crossing with no problems. Our wagon rolled onto the sandy river bank. We were there!

This was Malheur country. A closer look in the days and weeks ahead helped mama and me to see that this southeast part of Oregon had more to offer than we first thought. It was beef cattle and sheep country. As we moved along the trail, we saw forested hillsides. And the Malheur River flowed through much of it. I learned that many emigrant trains had traveled through here from Boise on their way to the Willamette Valley. We both began to like and appreciate it more.

Chapter IX

Several Years On the Malheur

Near the ferry crossing we met some cowboys driving cattle. They advised us to go on up by the Malheur River and look around. So we traveled twenty-five or thirty miles over a rough road made by cow herds and wagons. Late in the evening of the second day we came to a place by the Malheur River where we saw a large, fine-looking two-story house built of squared, rough chunks of stone. Near it were several very large wooden barns.

The road ran right past the house on one side and the barns, corral, bunkhouse and other outbuildings on the opposite side. This was the Rinehart ranch. It all looked very inviting, so papa arranged for us to camp nearby on the river bank. He soon got acquainted with the owner, Lou B. Rinehart, whom he liked from the start.

Mr. Rinehart showed him around the ranch. After a few days, he told papa he might need a partner later on, and would papa like to stop there indefinitely with his family and help on the ranch? They agreed on a plan for us to live with them at the ranch house. Mama and Mrs. Rinehart soon grew to be good friends.

The Rinehart family included two nice little boys, Arthur and Jimmie. Arthur was about two years younger than I. Jimmie was four. There also were the cowboys and a hired man, Mose, who did all the cooking. This was a big job, because the stagecoach changed horses at the big house, which served as the local inn. The driver and passengers usually stayed overnight. So did cattlemen passing through. The four or five "extra" bedrooms upstairs were nearly always filled with transients. We lived in the stone house for more than a year. Arthur became a very pleasant and enjoyable little playmate.

When settlers within many miles of the ranch heard that mama had taught school, they persuaded her to become their teacher in the one-room school several miles from the ranch house. She agreed and taught for two years. I was one of her pupils.

Papa filed under the Homestead Act for 160 acres of land about one mile up the Malheur river and near the cattle trail. He and mama set to work building a small, plain but substantial log house on an incline up from the river a little. Papa continued working for Mr. Rinehart.

By the early part of our second year at the ranch we were nicely settled in our new cabin, in among large, beautiful pine trees. The cabin consisted of a single large room, a big stone fireplace, a front window, and front and back doors. The floor was hard-packed dirt. Papa built a small bunk for me against the back wall near the fireplace, and a wider one for them at the front of the cabin. We used my bed as a lounge during the daytime, especially after the weather became colder, since it was near the fireplace. Mama had saved newspapers which came to the stone house, so she and papa used them to paper the cabin walls. They were careful to place all the papers right-side up so they could help me in learning to read. Every morning I had to learn to spell some of those smaller words before I could go out and play. That, and past lessons at Green River and along the Trail, were some of my earliest schooling. How I enjoyed learning those words. I remember the first long word I learned to spell and read was California. The paper I read it from was, I believe, the *San Francisco Call.*

One time, past midnight, mama was suddenly awakened by a bright light at one side of the fireplace. Somehow, the fire had burned under or around the fireplace wall. It had leaped to the papered wall and began to move along it toward my bed. She and papa jumped up and doused the blaze just in time. In another minute it would have had my blankets afire.

Mr. Rinehart spent much of his time now away from the ranch, though Mrs. Rinehart and the two boys stayed on at the stone house. He was having a big, new home built at Union, a community of about 600 people, located a little over 100 miles northwest from the ranch. It was for a while the County seat of Union County. Mr. Rinehart had decided to run for the State Senate, and he was beginning to organize his campaign.

We stayed on in the Malheur country for a total of about two-and-a-half years. Those were good years for my parents and me. Arthur and I played together around the ranch like brother and sister. We roamed the prairies looking for colored rocks, and we built play houses. My pet dog, Capers, which someone at the ranch gave me, was our constant companion. Sometimes Arthur and I would hike out on the prairie and have our lunch. We'd make a little sagebrush fire and bake, in the hot ashes, potatoes and eggs which we'd taken from home. Other times, we climbed up on the wooden corral pole fence and watched the cowboys branding steers. We scampered down in a hurry, though, when a bull headed toward us.

When the Rineharts moved away from the ranch, I cried and cried because Arthur and Jimmy were gone. Arthur had been the only child at the ranch around my age. To make me feel better, papa gave me a nice white pony we named Dexter. Because of my riding lessons back in Green River on that big livery stable horse, I soon felt fully at ease riding Dexter. Many days I was on that pony from morning until night.

I rode Dexter all over the ranch—bareback most of the time. Sometimes I used a surcingle, and at other times I rode side-saddle, which mama said was the proper way for a young lady. Most of the time I rode astride, which I liked best. I liked to ride Dexter at a flat-out run, even jumping irrigation ditches. I'd put my head forward and down. Mama said she'd look out the window and see me racing across the ranch. Suddenly she couldn't see my head any more. She'd worry that I fell off. Then, seconds later, she said, my head would reappear as we came up out of a slight dip in the land. After a while, I began trying to do some of the horseback tricks I saw cowboys perform. I even learned to stay on while Dexter stood on his hind legs, and I learned to lasso well enough to have the rope go over a fence post or the neck of a slow-moving calf.

I often played with a gentle colt, about seven months old at the time of this incident. One day I tied a pair of sharp spurs to his tail. Then I put a halter on his head, wrapped the loose end of the halter rope around my waist and led him around. The jangling of the spurs and the sharp edges of the rowels banging against his hind legs scared him. He started to run. fast.

"Whoa! Whoa!" I yelled at him as he pulled me along, causing me to take steps, mostly through the air, about five feet at a time. Papa heard my anguished cries. He came running to spot the trouble. By now the pony was traveling very fast and heading for the river. Papa ran after me, shouting to me to undo the rope wrapped around my waist. After some struggle, I managed to unwrap it, and the crisis was over. Another lesson learned.

Mama began to teach me to sew. I had a little doll I wanted to dress. Mama cut out clothes for her and showed me how to sew them together. She insisted that the stitches be right; if they weren't, I had to take then out and do them again until I had it right.

"We rip what we sew," she used to say. Then she'd laugh.

Those lessons in doing tasks right helped me the rest of my life. I tried to draw pictures, too. Here papa was my devoted teacher. Because of his great interest in drawing and his earlier aspirations to become an artist or actor, all the time I was growing up he kept watching and encouraging my interest in art.

Winters were long and cold in the Malheur country. Deep snow and biting winds made big snowdrifts. They covered up fences and sheds. People gathered at each other's houses for socials. At some of them, mama organized spelling bees. It was fun and made better spellers among children and adults. She also arranged musicals at several homes which had pump organs. Before the Rineharts left, we were happy to join their family circle on winter nights around the huge stone fireplace in their big sitting room.

The fireplace had large crane hooks in the back for

hanging black iron cooking pots. They often held delicious smelling soups, stews and pot roasts that simmered in them day and night. Big chunks of pine firewood, with pitch oozing from them, made a roaring blaze. Pine knots lasted the whole evening. A coal oil lamp made a soft glow across the room. It was a cozy feeling to sit snugly inside and listen to the wind whistling around the corners of the house, and to look out the window and sometimes see the snow falling softly.

We all enjoyed every minute of those winter night gatherings, with each person, in turn, expected to tell a story of some interesting personal experience. The weather was so cold in winter that our faces and the front of us would be hot, while our backs felt cold. Sometimes cowboys and overnight guests from the stage were invited to join us. On such occasions, we all sang together, and we listened to the cowboys and stagecoach drivers tell about some of their exciting work experiences.

Before guests retired to their cold bedrooms, and we walked back to our own cabin, Mose would bring in something to eat, along with lots of steaming coffee. The cold air seemed to increase its good aroma. Mose was an angel, and that was his name: Mose Angele.

Cows had to be milked every day, and Mose milked them and churned the milk to make butter. The Rineharts had a stone cellar deep underground, where all the milk, butter, and fruit in Mason jars were stored, along with vegetables and barrels of apples. Since the ranch was so far from town, it was necessary to buy in quantity. Thus, barrels of flour and sugar also were kept there.

In late winter warm chinook winds began to blow and cause the frozen river ice to start melting. Then one day, after a chinook blew hard, the ice would start breaking up into great chunks. They made roaring, grinding sounds that could be heard a half-mile or more away as the swollen river swept the chunks downstream. We were happy to see the ice breakup come. It meant that soon—by April—the warm sun of springtime would return to the Malheur. Irrigated parts of the valley would start turning green, and wildflowers would add bright colors and fragrances to the land.

After we'd been at the ranch about a year-and-a-half, as I recall, Mr. Rinehart—now Senator Rinehart—and his family moved from their new home in Union to the state capitol at Salem, where he took up his new duties, and Mrs.Rinehart worked as a clerk. He asked papa to stay on and continue to manage the ranch. Papa agreed and we moved into the stone house.

The Rineharts had one great sadness while they were still in Union and before their new house there was completed. They lost their beloved little Jimmy to diphtheria, which was a scourge in those times.

Many cattle and sheep men who drove their herds and flocks through the ranch often had in them a new-born calf or lamb. Since it would be too young to keep up with the older animals, sometimes an owner would say to me, "Maudie, I'll give it to you if you'll raise it on a bottle for your own."

"Oh, I'd love to have it!" I'd tell him.

Tickled to have the dear little pet, I began to think, after this happened three or four times, I'd like to have a little herd of my own some day. I had lots of fun, with much help from mama, raising them on a bottle filled with milk, and a nipple, just like bottles used to feed babies. My, how they would go for it! We had to feed them several times a day at first, while they were very young and frail. This went on until I had a herd of nineteen calves and lambs.

One calf used to bawl often and sounded exactly like it was saying, "Ma-a—m-a-a..." Baby lambs were harder to raise than calves. When we left the ranch we sold the herd for a tidy sum, which was put into a bank account in my name.

One day papa had a really severe earache, and mama was not right there at the time, so he handed me a bottle of turpentine and asked me to pour one drop into his ear. He sat on the floor while I tried to do exactly as he said. I must have become nervous, because I must have poured in many drops. He jumped up and ran out of the house, screaming. Everyone turned and ran to him to see what was wrong. I began screaming, too. I thought I had killed him. Someone called for Mama, who came quickly came and poured sweet oil into his ear. That eased his pain some.

On a hot afternoon in early July, 1881, papa, mama and I, along with the cowboys and domestic help, were sitting in front of the biggest barn, in the shade of a tree. We were carding wool, which the cowboys had just sheared from the sheep. A man approached on horseback. Even I noticed he looked upset. He told us President Garfield had been shot the previous day. Instantly, the lively spirit in our little group changed to sadness. When the newspaper arrived some days later, papa and mama read it aloud together with much interest to learn more about the assassination.

(On July 2, 1881 a disappointed office seeker shot President Garfield. The President lingered on until September 19, when he finally died.)

About six months after the Rineharts moved to Salem, papa and mama began to talk more and more often about the need for me to get into a bigger school for the years ahead, and to get on with their dream of settling in some beautiful green valley on a ranch of our own.

In the spring of 1883, we said our goodbyes to the ranch hands and other dear friends and widely scattered neighbors who had come to mean so much to us over the past two-and-a-half years. We loaded up our same old covered wagon once more, and again papa harnessed King and Sparkie, while Charlie trotted along behind. He changed places from time to time with one of the other two horses. We headed north and west on our way to the much-praised Willamette Valley. Some said the people there were called "webfooters" because of the heavy rainfall.

Papa had decided that on our way, we'd travel through Union in the beautiful *Grande Ronde* Valley, which they had been hearing described in such glowing terms by the Rineharts and many others passing through the ranch. It was supposed to be rich in productive soil and minerals. We were told that the *Grande Ronde* Valley floor is about 4,000 feet high. When mama heard that, she said she liked high altitudes. Since we'd be traveling over better roads than we came West on, papa thought we might make it in about a week to Union, where the Rineharts had built their new home. They had urged us to visit Union and stay in their house as long as we wanted to.

This time as our covered wagon started out, there were only two people on the high wooden seat in front. My pony, Dexter, had become such a good friend, I couldn't bear to part with him. Since I was now ten years old, papa agreed I was big and strong enough to ride him all the way from the ranch to Union, which I did. I enjoyed every day in the saddle on that trip.

Leaving behind us the relatively very dry country in that part of southeast Oregon, we went through a mountain pass after about five days, and began to emerge into greener, more developed country. This change took place gradually. We traveled through the thriving little community of Baker City, on the outskirts of which were fine looking farms and ranches. We saw more stands of forests as we moved north. And we saw more and more wildflowers: buttercups, bluebells, wild roses and wild grapevine. We found good campsites by clear streams, and there was more good grass. How delicious those camp meals seemed again.

Next, we went through North Powder, where there were more prosperous looking ranches. Besides cattle, some wheat, oats and barley were raised in this area. Finally we went through a place called Pyle Canyon. It was a small, narrow passage within the *Grande Ronde Valley*, and it formed the south gateway to Union. Here the mostly barren hills on either side of the road seemed high to a little girl. The canyon road was rocky and rough, and the wind blew hard.

We emerged after some hours from Pyle canyon, and began to see again the sweeping beauty of the wide *Grande Ronde* Valley floor. Now we could look a couple of miles to our left and see the Oregon Short Line Railroad being built. It was a continuation of the Union Pacific line. Large gangs of workmen were laying railroad tracks which would take trains around the big mountains forming the west side of the valley and on to the town of La Grande, about fourteen miles northwest of Union. Those mountains on the west side are tree-covered, and they are snow-capped part of the each year. They are part of the beauty of the *Grande Ronde Valley*.

Now out of Pyle Canyon on the north side, a wonderful surprise awaited us. We were ushered into one of the most beautiful parts of the whole *Grande Ronde Valley*: the area surrounding Union, and the town, itself. Before reaching the south end of town, we saw prosperous looking farms and ranches, with grazing horses and cattle, poplar trees, nice little streams, and a profusion of wildflowers. And we saw nice homes and barns. We continued on this road, and it led us right in to Union and along Main Street.

This was the Oregon country I believe mama and papa dreamed about. It certainly began to satisfy my own visions of what I had expected to see the day we ferried across the Snake River and onto the shore of southeast Oregon.

From the description the Rineharts had given us, we were easily able to locate their big, new home, in which they had hardly lived so far. It was on the south end of Main Street, before reaching the business district. We pulled into the yard and almost immediately Mose Angele, their faithful old servant from the Malheur stone house, came out and greeted us warmly. We stayed there in the house, empty except for Mose, for some days while we looked around the town and the valley. By the time papa and mama and I had unhitched the wagon and tied all four horses and went inside, Mose had a nice hot meal on the table for us.

The next morning not long after breakfast, and after papa and mama had asked Mose many questions about Union, the three of us walked up Main Street, which runs the length of the town. We soon reached the business district, among which were scattered some of the older homes and a few nice newer ones. We saw a very neat, thriving looking community, with the clear, fast-flowing Catherine Creek running the width of the town from east to west. The streets here, too, were lined with poplars. and a few maples. The homes looked comfortable and well-kept.

Nearly all the businesses at that time were on Main Street. On the left side, one of the first buildings we came to was the Methodist Church, built of wood and painted white. It was to become such a part of our life there. On both sides of the street were one and two-story buildings. Many were made of red bricks, but there were some frame buildings. We learned that the little bridge across Catherine Creek divided the business district from the north side residential area where, with some exceptions, most of the bigger, newer homes were. Here we saw bigger yards and more trees. It was at that time considered the "sweller" part of town.

As we walked up and down Main Street, both papa and mama were smiling broadly and talking enthusiastically with each other and me about what we were seeing. They were equally impressed with what they saw on some of the tree-shaded side streets, which were also part of the residential area, along with several more churches and a fine looking brick, two-story school. Two or three days later, after talking with many people in the town, all of whom seemed very friendly and welcomed us warmly, they decided to settle down here, at least for the time being.

How little I realized then what a big part this little community would have in shaping my life.

Chapter X

Girlhood in Union, Oregon

I was delighted with my parents' decision to settle down, at least for a while, in Union. The late spring weather, along with the beauty of apple and cherry trees in blossom, the nearby hills, the distant mountains, with their blue haze, rimming the valley, and the clear water of Catherine Creek flowing through the town, made my young heart feel in tune with life. Some of the peaks on the east side of the *Grande Ronde* Valley were still snow-capped. Most of the mountains were covered with pine and spruce, tamarack and other evergreen trees.

What a contrast this was to the endless, dry prairie lands, hot sun, sagebrush, dust, and strong winds we often had experienced along the trail to Oregon, and sometimes in the Malheur. Mama and papa shared my feelings that here was the Oregon we had dreamed about. Everywhere I turned, the little community seemed lush and green. Trees along Main Street helped give the town such a nice look.

Many homes in Union sat back some distance from the sidewalk and had nice lawns and big, leafy trees. Flowers around the yards were in bloom, giving off lovely fragrances.

During those first few days in Union, I saw many boys and girls along the streets and in their yards. Most of them smiled and said hello as I passed by. I had already learned years earlier in Saguache, Denver, and Green River that it was a Western custom for strangers to greet each other on the street.

On the third or fourth morning after our arrival, we had just finished a big breakfast Mose prepared for us. Papa said, "I'm going out today and look for a job." He and mama already had agreed that Union was a good base for looking around the *Grande Ronde Valley* for some ranch land.

When papa came back to the house for lunch, he said job opportunities looked good. He went out again after lunch, and returned within a couple of hours. This time he announced happily to mama, Mose and me that he had a new position. Mr. John Burns, who owned the only hardware store in Union, hired papa as a clerk and to keep the accounts. He had worked in a general store in both Petersburg, Illinois and Saguache, Colorado before taking the ranching job near Saguache, so he had good experience to offer.

Mr. Burns turned out to be a very gentle, kindly, and generous old bachelor. At least he seemed old to me at the time, though I learned later he had been only a little past forty when he hired papa.

The Rineharts' letter invited us to spend not just a few days, but to settle down and stay with them as long as we wanted in their big, new home when they eventually returned from Oregon's capitol at Salem. But mama said no, she felt strongly that we should go out and rent a house on our own. That's what we did.

Papa found a pleasant, four-room cottage close to Main Street, in the heart of the business section. It looked well-kept, and after we walked through it, papa pronounced it sound as a dollar.

I was particularly happy to see it had a big yard, which must have been more than an acre, so we could keep our horses there. Once again we loaded our few belongings into the covered wagon for the move to our new home. Like on the trip here from the Malheur, I rode Dexter, but this time the trip took less than a half-hour. Papa put the covered wagon in one corner of the back yard. He took off the canvas top and wooden, horseshoe-shaped ribs that had held it in place and stored them in the barn.

The first day we were in our rented house, Charlie, who had become such a pet of mama's and mine on our travel to Oregon, walked in the open front door, whinnying and trying to find us; then he went on down the center hallway and out the back door. Our dog, Capers, wasn't at the front of the house at the time or he wouldn't have let Charlie in. Capers howled almost all that first night. Mama decided he was homesick for the Malheur.

This block was owned by the town banker, Mr. W. T. Wright, and the home nearest us was occupied by him and his family. Mr. Wright was at that time having a very large new home built for him and his family across Catherine Creek in North Union. They had nine children, so they had outgrown their present home.

We still didn't have much furniture of our own, but my parents had been saving money ever since hey left Saguache, so they spent an exciting day ordering what we needed. Some of it had to be built by a local cabinet maker. I was so happy with a room all to myself. Mama made some nice, fluffy curtains for my bedroom window that looked out onto the front lawn, and she and papa got me a very nice, soft bed, a chest of drawers with flowers painted on them, a red chair, and pictures for the walls. For months, when I went to my room any time during the day, I'd open the window, look out and be happy all over again with the green lushness I saw in the yard and far beyond.

The only thing we didn't like was the way the wind blew dreadfully hard at times. It seemed to sweep up Pyle Canyon from the south and blow right through the valley.

One of the first things mama did when we were settled was to buy some pretty material and make me a nice new dress. When it was finished, she bought me a pair of shoes to go with it. She combed and brushed my hair out especially nicely that first Monday morning I was to start school. Then she walked with me over to the school and had me enrolled. It was a much bigger school than I had attended in the Malheur. I was at first awed by the size of it. Maybe that's because it was two stories high and made of brick. Each floor was divided into four rooms. Elementary school was on the first floor, with two classes to the room, and high school was on the second floor.

It was a great event in my life to go to school without mama there as teacher. I was embarrassed, though, when the nice teacher, Nellie Stephens, brought special attention to me that first morning by asking me to stand up, then introducing me to the entire class. At the first recess, three or four girls came up and spoke to me in a very friendly way. I began to feel myself relaxing from the tension I had built up because I was the new country girl in this big, modern school. That day I began to form some lifelong friends. Girls I met during that first recess introduced me to other girls and some boys that day and the days that followed. I began to enjoy Union Elementary from then on.

Frances "Fannie" Wright, eldest of the W. T. Wright's nine children, was my first and dearest chum in Union. The first time I ever saw her was the day we moved into their block. Mama sent me to her uncle Joe Wright's general store on an errand. While waiting there, I saw a small girl in a pretty white dress, playing a piano in the front of the store. She played wonderfully well for such a small girl. I thought, Gee, but don't I wish I could play like that girl. I told mama about her. She said, "Music is one of my plans for you, Maudie. You must learn to play like that little girl can. But it takes a lot of practice. You'll have to work hard. She worked hard to learn to play that well when she's so young. Some day we'll have our own home and a piano. Then you may take lessons."

Fannie's father was the leader of the town band. When he learned that papa could play the cornet, he invited him to join the band. Papa accepted the invitation gladly, and through it he developed many new friends. He also was making new friends through his work at the hardware store.

Mrs. Wright talked my parents into joining the Methodist Church. Soon she had mama singing in the choir. Through Fannie, I became well-acquainted with her brother, Will. He became my first beau in school. Fannie and I began going together to young people's church socials and other gatherings. We both liked to hang around the piano and sing.

Fannie also had a pony, so she and I rode often together through the town and up and down the valley. Sometimes we went out after school, but we rode mostly on weekends. There were two reasons for this. I had chores to do before dinner, and I had to buckle down and study in the evening.

Papa told me when I first got Dexter, that before taking him out I always must clean his hoofs and brush him out carefully so he looked his best. It would take twenty to thirty minutes to bring Dexter into the barn and groom and saddle him. In winter, because of the mountains on both sides of town, it got dark well before five o'clock. So during those months, Frances and I did our riding mainly on weekends.

Capers always ran along behind us. Through our ponies and Capers, we both became friends with a lot of people of all ages. It's a funny thing, I thought then and still do, that if a person is on horseback, even strangers seem to feel more friendly toward the rider. Capers and Dexter liked everyone they met. Union in the 1880's was a small enough town—about 600 people—so that we'd likely have come to know most of them anyway after a while. People in Union, probably like in most other small towns of that era, never locked their doors at night. Burglaries of homes in Union were almost unheard of.

Neighbor ladies began calling on mama shortly after we moved to Union. One day, after we'd been there some months, mama sat sewing while she and a visiting neighbor lady had coffee and talked. It came out during the conversation that mama had made the dress she was wearing. The lady was very impressed. Hesitantly, she asked mama if she would consider making a dress for her. Mama agreed. The lady was so pleased with the design and sewing that she told other ladies about it. That led to more requests from other women in Union.

There was no seamstress in town. Before agreeing to do any more sewing for other ladies, mama talked the matter over with papa. She told him she had plenty of free time, so she wanted to help earn money to help buy the ranch. At first, papa didn't like the idea. Like most men of his day, he thought the place of a wife and mother was in the home. She pointed out that she would be at home. Instead of having so much leisure time, she'd be sewing. Finally, he reluctantly

agreed. Word spread even wider about mama's designing
and sewing dresses for others. Soon she had more requests
than she could accept. So she hired a fine and very able young
lady, Mina Coffinberry, to help her.

The Rineharts came back to their big house in Union
after the legislature adjourned each year. Arthur and I easily
picked up where we had left off as playmates back in the
Malheur country. This caused some awkwardness for me,
since I now thought of Will Wright, still our next door
neighbor, as my special boy friend. I tried to tell Will that
Arthur and I were more like brother and sister. We had kind
of grown up together. While Arthur obviously regarded me
like a sister, I enjoyed Will's increased attention to me.

I continued to find life in Union altogether delightful.
I enjoyed high school—now I was on the upper floor—even
more than I had liked elementary school. Mama taught me
a little more each week about seamstress work, and I found
myself really liking it. I was proud when she complimented
me on some sewing task she thought I did particularly well.
Sometimes, though, I'd still try to go too fast, or not pay full
attention to what I was doing. Or maybe I'd visit too much
with one of my chums who might have dropped by. I'd make
mistakes. When mama saw them, she'd sometimes use, for
humor, the same little saying she taught me back at the
Malheur when I was only eight or nine, and learning to sew
doll clothes: "We rip what we sew!" Then we'd both laugh.

I had many fine girl friends in those years, though
Fannie remained my best friend. We often joined with other
young people our age in sledding and ice skating on the pond
in winter and horseback riding and picnics in the summer.
A few of the braver, hardier boys learned to swim in the
sometimes turbulent Catherine Creek, or they hiked out to
swim in lakes some distance from Union.

When we girls gathered around the piano or organ on Sunday evenings or at church dinners or parties in homes, a few boys might join in. Most of them, though, sat or stood nearby and simply listened. Maybe some boys thought they didn't have good enough voices. Others said they didn't know the words to many of the popular songs of the day.

My chores at home usually took up between one and two hours a day. I made my own bed, kept my room clean, and wiped the dishes which mama washed. Sometimes she filled the reading lamps with kerosene—some called it coal oil—after cleaning the glass chimneys. But when she was too busy, that job fell to me, too.

Papa also assigned me chores. Every day I saw that the water trough out by the barn was filled. This meant pumping water from the well with our iron hand-pump, and carrying it in tin buckets to the horse trough. In winter, I had to feed each of our horses hay. When they were working, or when the weather got especially cold, papa might ask me to feed them oats, too. When it snowed, it also was my job to shovel the walk from the front door to the sidewalk in front of our house. Papa did all the rest of the snow shoveling. When one of mama's out-of-town employees, who was learning to sew, lived in our home, then she and I shared some of those tasks.

From the beginning, papa got along well with Mr. Burns at the hardware store. Besides waiting on trade, he kept the accounts. Sometimes he brought the hardware accounts books home and worked on them evenings and weekends. Mr. Burns was not well from the time papa first began to work for him. He had Bright's Disease for many years. From time to time, he had to stay home because he just didn't feel well enough to come to the store. At such times papa would go to see him, and often mama would make some hot food for him.

Both Mr. Burns and papa were Masons. This, among other things, seemed to help make a strong bond between them. Mr. Burns also seemed to greatly enjoy his frequent visits to our home. Mama thought he was an unusually nice and kind man. I could see he thought mama was very nice, too. And he was very nice and friendly to me. Maybe it helped take place of children or grandchildren he never had.

One time, less than two years after papa started working for him, Mr. Burns became ill again. Only this time he seemed much sicker than usual. The doctor confined him to bed. One evening when papa dropped by for a visit with some hot dinner mama had cooked, Mr. Burns said to him, "John, I fear I'm never going to get out of this bed. I've been doing some thinking. I want to give you and Mollie a house I own. It has many nice fruit trees and a fine yard, so I think Mollie and Maudie and you will find it a good, comfortable place to live in."

When papa came home that evening and told mama and me what Mr. Burns had said about not having long to live and wanting to give a nice house to us, tears came to his eyes. Then mama and I began to cry. Mr. Burns must have written what he said about the house into his will, for when he died a few weeks later, my parents inherited the fine house on Main Street in North Union. It sat on two nice big lots. He also left some land in town to the Masonic Lodge, along with money to help build a new Masonic Temple. Mr. Burns had two sisters living somewhere else. Although he had left much of his estate to them, both of them contested the part of the will giving the house to us. But the court upheld the will.

We were overwhelmed by Mr. Burns' generous gift. It was a fine house, located on the west side of Main Street, two houses north of the bridge over Catherine Creek. I could look right out of the front of the house and see my chum, Fannie Wright's, new home about two blocks to the east.

Our house sat back from the street, with a nice lawn and shade trees. It had a big farm kitchen, with a nice cooking range. In the winter, one of my favorite places in the house was to sit on a chair on the side of that range, near where the wood was put in, while I read or sewed, and mama worked in the kitchen. By the time I was fourteen, though, I was doing almost as much as Mama to help make supper. This was fine with me. She was teaching me to cook, and I found that I really enjoyed it. Also, after sewing dresses all day, mama was tired.

The kitchen was big enough to hold a large, rectangular table, where we always ate breakfast. Often, in winter we ate all three meals there, too, because the kitchen always was so nice and warm. At one end of the kitchen was a walk-in pantry where mama could store on shelves all our food and most of our pots and pans. Next to the kitchen, on the opposite side of the house, was a small, separate dining room with a round table that could seat six. With extra leaves, it could seat four more. The sitting room—living room, we call it now—ran across the whole front of the house. A big brick fireplace was along one wall.

In those years, people seemed to spend so much more time doing things together in evenings—like reading aloud to each other, telling stories, singing, or families just having dinner together in each other's home and visiting. The fireplace was one of the focal points of the home in those years, at least in cold weather. Upstairs were a hallway and two big bedrooms, separated by several large hall closets. Like at the other house, my room was in the front, looking out on the lawn. I loved it. Soon I had it decorated with framed pictures of horses and pen and ink and water color sketches I had made—some with help from papa.

About thirty feet from the back porch we had a wooden privie. It was painted white. High up on either side, for air circulation, were tiny windows cut out in the shape of half-moons. Like in stories I heard many years later, our privie and those of our neighbors all seemed to have as standard equipment, a small pile of old newspapers.

After she had been sewing for others for about two years, mama became all excited one day over some news she'd just heard. The local millinery store was for sale. Some months earlier Grandma Knowles had sent her money which was from a government settlement related to mama's own papa's death resulting from severe health problems he contracted as a soldier in the Civil War. He had died from that sickness when mama was only twelve.

We had seen the store many times. It was nice looking and carried a fine stock of ladies' hats, gloves, scarves, and other accessories. Mama thought she had a good business head and that the millinery business would fit nicely together with her dressmaking.

She and papa talked it over that night for a long time after they retired. I could hear the muffled sounds of their voices. Sometimes papa's voice got loud and sounded stern; then it would drop down again. Mama must have been pretty persuasive, because the next evening after work, the three of us walked down to the shop. They talked for a while with the owner. In the end, my parents agreed to start taking inventory the next day. It wasn't long after that until I began stopping in more and more often and helping mama after school and sometimes on Saturdays. I found myself enjoying the work at the shop.

These were very happy growing up years for me.

Occasionally, papa got mad at mama or me or some situation at work, and showed that temper he still had trouble keeping under control. But, like a dark rain cloud, it would soon pass and the normal atmosphere of peace and happiness resumed in our home. While mama was blessed with a sweet, easy-going temperament, she could be firm and steadfast regarding what she considered important matters. This was displayed in things like her strong desire to see me become a well-educated young lady, her help through the years in saving to buy a ranch, and in the way she developed her sewing and millinery business.

With the growing demand for dressmaking, she added that business to the shop. She always kept the best dressmaker she could find to help her run it. Before mama bought the shop, she had several girls in town working with her to learn dressmaking. They and a couple more girls in town joined her in the shop. Sometime she took a girl from out of town to learn the business. That girl would live at our house. I made some fine friends that way. It was part of mama's sunny nature to smile readily and have a cheerful word for everyone. I believe that was one of the things that helped make her business grow. People just felt good being around her, and some ladies told me that. After a while, she carried everything needed in a ladies' store.

By the time I was fifteen, many of my girl friends and some of their mothers began commenting on how young and beautiful my mother looked. She was only thirty-one. I was much more aware of her appearance than I had been a few years earlier. Standing about five-feet-four, and very well-proportioned, her sea blue eyes formed a pleasing contrast with her thick chestnut brown hair and flawless skin and complexion. I was proud of mama's nice appearance and her nice ways. I was especially pleased when someone remarked occasionally that mama and I looked quite a bit alike. I determined to try to be like her in temperament, too.

From the time we first moved to Union, papa had continued to take great interest in my efforts to sketch. He still took time to study each picture carefully, and he always had encouraging comments. Even when I could see he wasn't impressed with a particular effort, he found something good to say about it, and he made helpful suggestions for improving the next one.

"Maudie," he'd sometimes say, "stick with it. Some day you'll be the fine artist I always wanted to be."

Chapter XI

Happy Teen-Age Years

I thought our little town of Union in the Oregon of the 1880's couldn't be nicer. Even as a young teen-ager, I knew it was a fine place to live. My parents seemed to like it as much as I did. But now, though, I seldom heard them talk about buying a ranch somewhere in the Grande Ronde Valley. After Mr. Burns had died, his business was closed out. Papa and Mr. David Layne eventually joined together to organize a new hardware store. Like papa, Mr. Layne knew the business thoroughly, and they got along well together.

I was happy in school. I counted many of my classmates as good friends. And my closest chums and I liked all but one of our teachers. Among my dearest friends in those school years were Fannie Wright, Jeanette McGillis, Emma Seamans, Carrie Skiff and Mabel Carter. Our teachers gave me the feeling that they liked me and wanted to help me do my best with my lessons and as a girl growing up. I know my chums felt the same way, and I imagine the rest of the students—at least those who took time to study, did, too.

My teachers' attitudes toward me re-enforced my good feelings for them. In the years since finishing school, I have always seemed to do my best when working with people who, I saw or sensed, liked me and transmitted to me—often unspoken—their confidence that I could do well whatever task was at hand.

Still, we girls did our share of complaining about having to spend one to two hours on homework every night except on weekends. As I grew older, my home chores and those of my school friends increased. We sometimes complained to each other about that, too. Many families in Union lived on an acre or more of ground at the edge of town, and kept a cow and a horse or two. There were no cars in those days. The horses pulled buggies, farm-type working wagons, and in winter some pulled sleighs or big sleds. Boys split wood and kindling for the kitchen range and the parlor stove or fireplace. They cleaned barns and chicken houses, milked the cows and helped their fathers feed the livestock. If there were no boys in the family, or if they had too many other chores, the girls pitched in and helped with that kind of work, too.

Often as not, as in my case, girls churned milk into butter and made whipped cream. By the time we got into our teens, we were helping our mothers with the cooking, baking and sewing, unless they had a hired girl to do it. Very few families in town did.

Sometimes I wished I had a brother or sister or both, to keep me company and to help with chores. Among my other tasks was to carry in wood that papa split. Like other boys and girls, I helped plant and weed the family vegetable garden. In summer I helped harvest the vegetables and pick fruit from the trees.

Anyway, we didn't think of our after-school jobs as unusual. It was customary for young people growing up in a small town before the turn of the century. Looking back, I can see it built into us good work habits and taught us skills that came in handy when we grew up. Even with our chores and school homework, my chums and I all had enough time to play.

What crazy things we school girls and boys could think up to do. We were high-spirited and brimming with energy, and we came up with our share of light-hearted stunts. Once several of my girl chums and I found some old skirt hoops in a trash box behind one of the stores downtown. Hoop skirts were just going out of fashion in Union, but that didn't register with us. We were delighted with this find. We hid them in some bushes on the way to school.

That night without our mothers' knowledge, we fixed the hems of our skirts so a wire hoop could slide through them. The next morning on the way to school, we retrieved the hoops and threaded them through the hems in our skirts. Then we walked on to school, stepping high and proudly, feeling we were in top fashion. Other girls squealed with delight and admiration as they saw the startling new touch to our attire. Boys grinned and laughed with appreciation. We sneaked into our seats before the teacher entered the room.

How embarrassed we became a few minutes later when our teacher asked part of the class, including my chums and me, to come to the front of the room and sit on the floor in a big half-circle in front of her desk. Then we had to take our turns to stand and recite the lesson. We quickly came to realize that if we failed to sit back down just right, up came the front of our skirts. The stiff wire in front of our skirts almost hit us in the chin, while little was left to be imagined about the kind of undies we were wearing. We never tried that again!

Our desks were double width, so we each had a seatmate. Once my chum, Emma Seamans, and I shared a seat. Emma had beautiful thick, chocolate brown hair and brown eyes. My hair was chestnut brown and I have blue eyes. For several weeks she and I had discussed changing the color of our hair. Somewhere we got the idea that a bottle of ammonia liberally rubbed into our hair would transform both of us into beautiful blondes. We bought a small bottle of ammonia in town, and hid it in our desk the next day.

Each morning for three days we would duck under the desk when the teacher stepped out of the room, and rubbed the ammonia into our hair. We didn't get very far with our make-over plans, however. On the third morning, our teacher walked past our desk. She paused a second or two as she went by and sniffed. Then she turned around after a few more steps, came back to our desk, and sniffed again. Then she studied our damp hair, leaned over and smelled it. Gently but firmly, in the presence of our grinning and highly amused classmates, she drew from us a confession about our plans to become blondes. With a trace of a grin, she extended her hand, and we, blushing with embarrassment, handed the ammonia bottle to her.

Because my parents made me study every evening, I knew my lessons well at school. So I found time to do some sketching on my own. At those fairly frequent times when the teacher assigned our geography class to draw maps of different countries, some of my nearby classmates asked me to sketch theirs, too. I also amused myself by sketching my classmates' portraits. But one day I "got in bad" with my drawing. On that particular day, a school board member made one of his periodic visits. He was so homely that some of us students unkindly named him "It." There he sat on the platform near the teacher, living up to his reputation with us. I quickly sketched his likeness, to the amusement of several students sitting near me. Our teacher, a man, noticed I was creating a distraction and said, "Maude, what are you doing?"

"Nothing," I answered.

But those students sitting near me didn't help at all by continuing to look over at my slate with big grins and a few audible chuckles. The teacher said, "What do you have on your slate?"

"A sketch," I replied.

"Come up here and put your sketch on the blackboard, just as you have it on the slate," he ordered sternly.

So I had to do it. In transferring it to the board, I tried to change it enough so that Mr. "It" wouldn't recognize himself. But when I gazed at the completed drawing, I was certain I had failed. The school board member would recognize it and the fat would be in the fire.

The teacher studied it briefly, then scolded me sternly, though I detected the shadow of a tiny smile while doing so. He said I had to remain after school for a "curtain lecture." When we were alone after classes were dismissed, he gave me a severe scolding, all right, though again he couldn't hold back a tiny smile while delivering it.

Sometimes, because of our high spirits and silliness when we girls got together, we'd do things of which we were later ashamed. One of these incidents involved dear old Mr. Swackhamer. I was probably fifteen at the time.

It happened one Sunday morning during communion. The church was so quiet you could hear even a whisper. Fannie, Mabel, Jennie and I were sitting close together in one pew. It was not secured to the floor. We had learned from previous unfortunate experiences that when we got to laughing quietly—we hoped—among ourselves, we made the pew shake. This caused a loud noise in the otherwise very hushed atmosphere. More than once, our mothers had strongly reprimanded us about such conduct in church. We knew it was wrong. Most of the time we managed to keep our exuberance under mild control. Not this morning.

Mr. Swackhamer was a dear old man, around ninety. He was a near neighbor and a pillar of the community. He had such a kind, gentle manner, and he was generous in so many ways that he was beloved throughout Union. This particular morning he knelt by the rail to receive communion. He rested his right hand on the polished wooden rail and, because he had palsey so badly, the big ring on his finger banged steadily against the rail and echoed loudly throughout the church.

We girls looked at each other and began to giggle. Our bodies shook with pent-up mirth. Soon one of us emitted a small, audible laugh. The rest of us looked at her and responded in kind. This led to a new outburst of giggling which surely could be heard plainly by those in a half-dozen pews in front and back of us. Soon our loose-standing pew began to shake. It made considerably more noise in the otherwise quiet church than Mr. Swackhamer's ring. The dear old man seemed completely unaware that we were giggling at him.

Mrs. Wright frowned at us from up in front with the choir, and she motioned for us to leave. The second we reached the sidewalk, we burst into uncontrollable laughter. Each of us received a strong, well-deserved reprimand from our parents when they later had us home alone.

The pace of life in Union was pleasantly slower in those

years. There was something very satisfying about it. Sometimes I think it would be nice if we could keep the best of our modern things—like greatly improved medical care, better transportation and communications, and greater equality for women—we didn't even have the vote then—but still have that slower, gentler way of life. There was more time back then for family togetherness and for visiting with friends and neighbors.

The most common kind of social activity, besides gatherings at churches and lodges, was visiting with another family. When one family invited another for supper, it nearly always included all the children—and families were bigger in those years. After dinner, which usually included lots of lively talk, the men moved to the parlor while the ladies and older girls did the dishes and cleaned up in the kitchen, and the younger children played. When we were all together again in the parlor, we'd join in more talk, and there usually was some story-telling.

If the host family happened to have a hand-pumped organ or a piano or mandolin, the mother or older child might play, and maybe we'd all sing together. Some families also had stereopticon photo projectors. Then they'd treat us to pictures projected against the wall or onto a sheet pinned to the wall. We'd see Niagara Falls, the ruins of Athens or Pompei, and the like. Around ten o'clock, one of the visiting parents would say, "Well, it's getting late, and already it's past the kids' bedtime..."

But we also had our community problems in those earlier years. It was much too common for someone to get a bad cold, then end up dying of pneumonia. Doctors didn't seem to know very much about causes of heart problems, so many people died suddenly of heart attacks. Nor did they seem very able back then to cope with appendicitis. A burst appendix was usually fatal. Tuberculosis was a scourge, and TB sanitariums were a common institution in larger towns.

Although divorces did occur, they weren't at all common, and they were looked upon by the rest of the community as a tragedy. When young ladies and men got married, their attitude seemed to be that they were making a life-long commitment. But because even then, people had their frailties, sometimes a man deserted his wife—occasionally a whole family—by simply walking away from them and never being heard from again. However, the great majority of the people seemed to live happy, normal lives, with loving families and fine friends. Women simply didn't smoke cigarettes. On rare occasions when we heard about some woman who did, it was likely a reference in a newspaper or magazine about some well-known actress or other celebrity in a distant large city who smoked. Even that shocked us.

By the time I was sixteen, my chums and I were allowed to go to parties, but on those few occasions when the parties were on a week night, we were expected to be back home by 10:00. On Friday and Saturday nights we could stay out until 10:30. One time we were having such a good time at the home of one of my closest friends, that it was after 11:00 before any of us—including her parents—noticed the time.

The doorbell rang, and there were my parents. I was terribly embarrassed. They had come to take me home. Within minutes, several other parents showed up, concerned about their children being out late. A very nice young man by the name of George Benson, who had taken a special liking to me, had escorted me to the party. He walked back with us to our home and didn't show any evidence of embarrassment or resentment toward my parents for not leaving it up to him to get me safely home.

As we moved up into our upper teens, Fannie and I

still rode our horses together around the valley. We did this less often now, though, because I spent more time after school and on Saturdays at mama's shop. In winter, my crowd of boys and girls often gathered to ice skate at the frozen millpond behind the dam. We enjoyed many evenings there in fine, wholesome fun. No rowdies or toughs were allowed on or near the pond. It was uncommon for high school boys to smoke. Those few who did were frowned upon, and I never saw a high school boy take a drink.

When the winter's ice melted and the valley began to blossom again, many young people shifted from ice skating to roller skating over at Wright's Hall. Someone started a dancing school in Union, which many of my crowd attended for a while and enjoyed greatly.

There was no electricity in Union until 1890, when I was seventeen. Papa had lights put in our house about a year later. And there were no movies or radios. We had been hearing for several years around the time we arrived in Union about a fairly new invention called a telephone, but, as I recall, only a few began to show up in some of the business places during my high school years. We didn't have one and most of my friends' homes didn't. I think Fannie's family had a telephone, since her father probably needed phones in his bank, too.

Sometimes the Masonic Lodge or the Knights of Pythias would put on a play or musical program and the whole town turned out. Since my parents and some of my chums' mothers and fathers took part in planning and putting on such affairs, we attended these and often saw there other girls and boys in my crowd.

A popular kind of money-raiser that different organizations put on from time to time was a basket social. Each lady prepared a basket, decorated with bright-colored crepe paper, and maybe with bows or flowers. It would be filled with two delicious dinners. The baskets were placed on a table in front of the hall. Men and older boys then bid for the basket they wanted.

Part of the excitement in bidding was that no bidder was supposed to know who owned any of the baskets. The boys we knew were imaginative and interested enough, though, to develop a fairly effective spy network. Then when each basket was auctioned, a young man would bid strongly for the basket of the young lady he most admired at the time. Occasionally, however, his intelligence source erred, and he ended up having a fine dinner with a middle-aged matron. This kind of outcome brought lots of smiles and amusement from those who knew the young bidder was going to be in for a big surprise. The more alert young men, when they saw a lady's husband bidding strongly for the same basket, realized their error and quickly dropped out of the contest.

We never believed in dreams in my family, but the day came when all three of us had to reassess our views in the matter.

Chapter XII

A Dream Comes True

One morning when I awakened, I recalled vividly a dream I'd had the night before. As soon as I dressed and went down to the kitchen, I told mama I dreamed we received a letter from Grandma Knowles and Grandpa Knowles, saying they were coming to visit us. Papa's twin sister, Lydia Dowell and her daughter, Mollie—my eighteen-year-old cousin— were coming with them. While neither mama nor I really believed in dreams, this time we thought there might be something to it.

She sent me to the post office right after breakfast. There was no letter. The next morning she sent me again. Sure enough, there was a letter from East Greenview, Illinois, in grandma's handwriting. It said they were leaving in a few days, and papa's sister, Lydia, and my cousin Mollie were coming with them. It was now early autumn, 1887, and we had been in Union about four-and-a-half years. We had not seen them since the spring of 1880, when mama and I took the train from Ogden to their home in Illinois. It was a very happy and exciting day for all of us when the train rolled into the depot, two miles from Union, and there they were!

Every day was full of excitement as we visited with my grandparents, cousin Mollie, and Aunt Lydia in our home, and took them around to see the sights. We still had our horses, so papa rented a surrey—a buggy with two cushioned seats. Papa took time off from the hardware store, and we drove our visitors all over the Grande Ronde Valley. While Fannie and I had ridden all over it within about five miles in either direction from Union, there were many sights neither my parents nor I had seen. So our trips were great adventures for all of us.

Hot Lake, about six miles north of Union, and near tall mountains on the west side of the valley, was remarkable. One third of the lake boiled up in big bubbles. The water contained many minerals, including sulfur. When rings or other jewelry were dipped into the water, they turned black. There were three or four bathhouses built out over the water near the part of the lake that boiled. Many people believed that bathing in that water helped cure rheumatism and certain other medical problems.

Friends had told us that in the hottest part of the lake, eggs could be cooked just right in three minutes. While packing our picnic lunch, mama decided to test that information. She had put enough raw eggs in the picnic basket for all of us. During lunch, she placed them in a dish towel tied to a long stick, and dipped them into the lake. Grandpa took out his vest pocket watch and kept time. Sure enough, grandpa pronounced, after testing them, they were cooked just right.

The far side of the lake was cool. Even wild ducks

and geese swam around in it. The owner of the property had provided rowboats for guests. We spent the afternoon in one of them. We were mighty careful to steer clear of the boiling parts of the lake, because some time before, a boat had capsized over the boiling hot places and occupants were scalded to death before help reached them.

The new Oregon Short Line Railroad ran right through La Grande, about fourteen miles north of Union, making it a thrifty young community. It was already competing strongly with Union. While visiting there with the folks, papa told us, "La Grande will steal most of Union some day." He was pretty much right. A few years later some businessmen moved up there because it was on the rail line. And it took the county seat away from Union. But Union remained headquarters for the big stockmen in the valley and it continues to have many lovely homes.

Mama's folks were so pleased with Union and enjoying their visit so much, they decided to extend their stay. We had many good locally-provided things to eat, including deer and antelope, fresh red salmon caught in Catherine Creek, and fresh trout from nearby mountain streams. From the orchard we could pick, in season, fresh cherries, apples, pears, and plums.

Stock raising was the main work in the valley. Mama and papa had become well-acquainted in past years with several big ranch families, including the McAllisters and the Stewarts. When they came to town, they often made their headquarters at our home. Sometimes on Sundays we'd go out there and spend the day. I loved the ranches, with their big corrals, barns, and other outbuildings, and lots of horses around. The beef cattle often were grazing away from sight of the ranch house. Mama, Mrs. Stewart and Mrs. McAllister were close friends and always had so much fun when they were together.

When the folks wanted to visit a ranch, we took them to the Stewart's place. There they could see a real working outfit, and eat a superb ranch dinner. Mr. Stewart told the folks about the old-time freight wagons with high wooden sides and big wheels and drawn by four or six-horse teams. They had traveled through Union and up and down the valley hauling cargo right up until around the time we got there. That's when the Oregon Short Line came in, and there was no more need for them. Some of them were known as Conestoga wagons.

Many people in later years saw pictures of them and thought they were the kind of covered wagons most people traveled in over the Oregon Trail. But that wasn't the case. Most people came in much lighter wagons. Many had been regular farm wagons. Some rode in buggies and surreys, which might be part of a covered wagon family's outfit. A surrey or buggy could never have traveled alone. Room was needed for supplies, household items, and tools and materials for repairs. The big wagons were used mainly for heavy freight hauls. We had seen them often passing through the Malheur.

After the Short Line came in, a new form of diversion for some Union people, young and old, was to go two miles to the depot and watch the trains arrive and depart: see who was coming in and leaving town, and what kind of freight was unloaded. Horses around Union, unaccustomed to being near the loud noise of trains, sometimes became frightened by those big, noisy steam locomotives. Occasionally a horse or team would bolt and the driver had the terrifying experience of trying to cope with a runaway in a crowded area.

Mama's ranch friend, Adelia Stewart, seeing my strong interest in horses when we visited their ranch, began to teach me many new things about handling horses. She had a reputation as an expert horsewoman. Because of her teaching, I became very confident in handling a horse under harness, and I became a better horseback rider.

Mama's parents ended up staying with us over a year. While Aunt Lydia had to leave after three months, cousin Mollie was having such a great time that she wanted to stay on, and she remained with us for two years. Everyone liked Mollie's sweet and lively disposition. The older group of young people—three or four years older than my crowd—invited her to many of their parties. Several young men wanted to escort her. I often carried notes from some of the boys to her and her replies to them.

Mollie was a fine pianist and organist. Often she was called upon to play the organ at church and the piano at parties. One day she told mama and me that back in Illinois she had suffered often with headaches and colds. After being in Union only a few months, she no longer had either. She said she had been thinking it might have something to do with the fact that she was so much happier out here in Union than back in Illinois.

I thought about that observation many times as the years went by. It does seem that when we are happy and feel all is going well, we also feel our best physically. It also seems that when grown people, anyway, get sick, it is often following some sad or tragic experience or when they are unhappy or depressed about something. Maybe our sense of well-being, or lack of it, does indeed affect us physically.

When the folks were getting ready to leave after their long visit with us, they were very anxious to have me return with them and spend a year at their farm. I didn't want to leave my parents and all my friends in Union. But they persisted strongly, so mama and papa told me they thought that for grandma's and grandpa's sake, I really should go.

In the end, I went back with them on the train and spent a year in Illinois. I made many new friends there, though I spent a lot of time writing to my family and chums in Union. I could hardly wait to return home. Among my new acquaintances in Greenview were a number of nice boys, and I was invited out repeatedly by several of them.

One very nice young man, Arthur, who was about three years older than I and worked for a newspaper, took a special liking to me and I began to feel the same toward him. Grandma was very strict with me. Most of the time I felt, in that respect, almost like a prisoner in their home. She practically forbade me to see Arthur. Yet when the local banker's son invited me out, grandma approved right away. He drank quite heavily and for other reasons I didn't care for him. When my school year was up, I was simply delighted to travel back to Union and pick up where I had left off with my family and friends.

Mama and papa, along with some of my chums met me at the station. Among these were the ones I'd been closest to: Fannie, Emma, Jennie, and Mabel. Carrie's parents had both died, and Carrie no longer lived in town. The five of us picked up right where we left off. I was now seventeen, and felt that life couldn't be better.

I didn't know at the time that within the next few months I'd be faced with one of the biggest decisions in a young lady's life.

Chapter XIII

I Become Engaged

The first morning after returning home from Illinois, I awakened in my room to find the sun streaming in, the sky bright blue, and birds chirping in the yard. I lay there a minute reveling in being back home. My exuberance overflowed, and I let out a squeal of joy. Mama, who was just going down to make breakfast, came down the hall to my room, opened my door a crack and looked in.

"Did you call, Maudie?"

"Oh mama, I'm just so happy to be back home!" I said.

Mama laughed and walked over to my bed and hugged me tightly. I saw tears in her eyes.

"We missed you so much," she said, sniffling. Then tears came to my eyes.

Right after breakfast I went out to the back yard for a reunion with my pony, Dexter, and the other horses. Dexter and Charlie whinnied as soon as they saw me enter their pasture. King and Sparkie simply walked over to me so they could be petted and have the tops of their manes scratched. For a long time I petted, scratched, and talked to them. Then, walking back to the house, I stopped and stood for a minute, breathing in that pure, fresh air, feeling the sun on my face, and looking over at our house. I had already seen my cat, Pooh Bah. Several years before, I had lost my dog, Capers.

Within the next hour or two our house filled with my girl chums. The place soon rang with excited chatter and laughter. There were Frannie and Emma, Jennie and Mabel, Ella Green, Anna and "Fudge" Hanna and others. Mama had already decided to take the day off from the store. She invited them all to stay for dinner. We call it lunch now.

In the afternoon we all walked downtown. Union seemed to have hardly grown at all. They told me George Benson had been asking about me and that he hoped he could see me soon. He had written to me quite often while I was away. We returned home later to sit in the shade of a big tree on the lawn and talk and laugh and sing all our favorite songs until nearly supper time, when they left for their own homes.

The second morning I was home, mama took me with her to her shop. There I was warmly greeted by the girls who worked for her and were more like part of our family: Jennie Benson, Lora Warren, Mina Coffinberry, and Ada Powers. George Benson, who was now working full time for Frank Hall, the Postmaster, dropped in to see me at the shop. He asked if he might come calling soon, which he did. After a few days back home, it seemed almost as if I'd never been away.

Now, when mama and papa and I sat down at the dining table, it seemed lonely to me. For more than a year before I went to Illinois, grandma and grandpa and cousin Mollie Dowell were all seated around the table with us. I missed this greatly. Mollie had gone on from Union to Grants Pass, Oregon, in the Rogue River Valley, where her father, Uncle Pete, had taken up a mining claim near the town.

Mama and I never grew tired of talking together. We chatted hour after hour and were the most loving companions. Back in Greenview, I had become quite fond of a young newspaper reporter named Arthur. After some months he started to get serious about me. In those years young people often got engaged and married earlier than they do today.

Soon after I was back home I had told mama about Arthur and how he wanted to write to me. She said I was too young to be taking a boy seriously, and to know my own mind. She asked me to promise I wouldn't correspond with him. She said I should concentrate on finishing high school and maybe even go on to college. I didn't want to stop writing to Arthur. I pleaded with mama to let me answer his letters. But in the end I reluctantly promised. Both my parents had drilled into me from the time I was small that I must always keep my word. I've tried to do that all my life.

During one of George's calls on me at home, we sat out on the lawn talking. He told me he wanted to be my steady beau. I didn't want a steady beau yet. Mama thought George, who was three years older than I, was about the nicest young man in town, and in different ways she clearly let me know it.

Shortly after I had returned home, Fannie Wright gave a lovely party. When George invited me, she urged me to go with him. So I did, and we had a good time together. After that, I kept on going to all the other "doings" with him. He would even come by on Sundays and take me to the Methodist Church, which my crowd always attended.

I'd have to leave George sitting in a pew while I went up in front and sang with the choir. If I didn't go up and join it, Mrs. Wright would come to wherever George and I were sitting and ask me to go with the choir, which mama now directed.

I was surprised at how fast the first year back home went by. It seemed like no time—maybe because it was such a full and happy one for me. My high school studies, home chores, working part-time for mama at the shop, riding Dexter, and taking part in church and all the small-town social activities continued to be big parts of my life then.

By the time I was eighteen, in January, 1891, mama and I were close to the same size. She was a bit heavier and an inch or two taller. Many people still remarked on how much we looked alike. Some of our friends said mama looked so young she could be mistaken for my sister. But for all her youthful looks, she had a fine head for business, and her millinery shop, including her dressmaking and hatmaking, were thriving. She had even opened shops in two nearby towns as outlets for extra materials and other items from the store.

George was pretty much my steady beau by now. Friends seldom invited one of us without the other. He would take me riding in a fine sleigh drawn by one of his family's beautiful, spirited bay horses. One night while we were on a ride out on the edge of town, we were talking so animatedly together that George didn't see a small bridge. When the sleigh struck one side of it, over we went. The sleigh turned over completely, spilling us out into the deep snow. When he finally got it right-side-up and the horse straightened out, we were so cold—the temperature was far below zero—we drove directly to my house. Papa built a red hot fire in the fireplace so we could dry out.

That summer eighteen young people in our crowd went camping, with two older married couples for chaperones.

George was my escort on the trip. Every summer different groups of young people, always with escorts, went camping in the Blue Mountains of the Grande Ronde Valley.

When at home, George would come to our house every Sunday afternoon. Usually, he and I went driving up Catherine Creek canyon, because it was so beautiful. Sometimes Jennie and Miles Carter, George and I, would go in Miles' surrey. And sometimes the four of us would take long walks on Sundays. It was all a lot of fun.

But there was a thorn among the roses. One of my girl acquaintances often tried in various ways to get George to go with her, since she had no beaus, and she clearly thought George was very nice. Sometimes she invited him over to her house on Sundays, but didn't invite me. George wouldn't go unless I was invited, too.

George had told me a number of times that he loved me. When I didn't answer that I loved him, too, he once said, "Maudie, you don't love me. Now tell me again I'm too good for you—isn't that it?"

I would say, "Oh, now, George, it could never be that. I do admire you and love you. But I can't get crazy about you."

"Well, it's all too deep for me," he'd answer.

Finally, George proposed to me one Sunday afternoon on our way back from a delightful buggy drive up the valley. I hardly knew my own heart, though I had grown very fond of him. He was clearly such a well-brought-up young man from a very fine family. He had a fair complexion, large, dark blue eyes, blonde hair, a slightly pug nose. He was tall, very slender, and very energetic. I thought he was very wholesome, good-looking, and a young man of fine instincts. He was the "pick of the town" and I knew it. But I could never bring myself to get crazy about him.

"I'll be very happy to be your wife, George," I said with a strong, warm feeling. "I know you well enough to know you'll always be dear and true to me."

"Yes, you know I will, Maudie," he said with emotion. "You know how true Alta and Sam are to their wives, and we boys in our family are all alike. I could love only you—always!"

I knew George meant every word of it. Once he said to me, "I'd never marry any other girl if anything should happen that we don't marry. I'd always be a bachelor." He was one in a million. Mama loved him, and she knew his true worth.

About that time, for the first time in my life, a dark cloud began to form over my head, and it wouldn't go away.

Chapter XIV

Tragedy Strikes

Papa had never been very demonstrative with mama and me. But now he was constantly upset, edgy, and curt with us. One morning mama told me he was going on a short trip to Portland. Her eyes were red, like she'd been crying. Papa took that trip, but when he returned there was no joy in our house. The tension seemed to get worse. He was, if anything, more upset and so was mama.

What's going on? I wondered. I was getting very tense and scared. This was so different from anything I had ever known. I couldn't understand any of it.

Then mama told me that when papa was in Portland he bought, against her will, two city lots and an acre in one of the city's suburbs. He wanted us to move to Portland.

This greatly upset mama. At first she argued that 1891 was a hard year, as a business turndown was affecting some parts of the country, including eastern Oregon. It was no time to make a change. Now, night after night when they were in their bedroom, I couldn't help hearing muffled sounds of his angry voice and mama's anguished responses.

One morning mama told me papa was determined to sell our house. We were to move temporarily into the little apartment in back of mama's shop. He was going to get rid of the horses and cow. Mama burst into heartbreaking sobs as she told me this, and she cried almost inconsolably when she had finished.

I held her in my arms a long time, and I shook with fright. My happy little world was crumbling. For several days mama refused to sign the papers to sell the house. She told papa this was her home and mine, too, and she didn't want to leave it or Union and all our friends and ties to the community. But papa persisted strongly. Finally, she signed the papers.

As soon as some of our close friends learned that papa was going to move us to Portland, they advised mama not to sell our home or her business and not to leave Union. Mama was so distraught, she didn't know what to do. She and papa had always seemed to be able to talk out their problems and reach decisions they could both accept.

Now to take the reins in her own hands against papa's wishes was something she most strongly wished to avoid, for her whole heart was wrapped up in him. How could she go against him? Wives seldom did that in those days. But she did, as far as our home was concerned. She walked right across the street from her shop to the bank and made arrangements to buy it back.

"It's my home and Maudie's, too," she said. "If Johnny wants to give it up, he can do so." That day she purchased it back. When papa learned what she had done and wouldn't agree to move to Portland, he stormed around like a mad animal. He kept telling her how foolish she was, while her friends were saying to one another how wise and level-headed she was, and that she was an excellent business woman.

Sunday, October 4, 1891, was mama's thirty-fifth birthday. She said she wasn't going to church that morning, but she wanted me to go. That worried me, because mama almost always went to church, unless she was sick, which was seldom. I can still remember that I wore a dark blue dress with a deep cream yoke and collar. I felt very lonely sitting in church that morning. Something inside made me feel very blue. I could hardly make myself sing. I knew it was because mama was so upset and wasn't here.

I began to wish I had stayed home with her. These days our home—at least temporarily—was the little apartment back of the shop. Papa had moved us out of our home and into the shop some weeks earlier. I felt like crying, but I remained until the services were over. Then I fairly flew back to her, not even waiting for the usual handshaking. When I reached the shop, mama said, "Why, Maudie, you're home early. Is church out?"

I kissed her and said, "Yes, mama, church is out. But when you weren't there, I missed you so much, it made me blue to think I left you—on your birthday, too."

"Oh, that's nothing, honey," she said. "I'm not counting any birthdays now. But we'll spend the day together, won't we? Your papa wants us all to go to the hotel for dinner."

After dinner at the hotel, papa walked back with us to the shop apartment, then left. Mama and I sat together for a long time in the living room and talked over many things. One subject was Arthur, the young man I'd met in Illinois. While she was sure Arthur was a fine young man, she preferred George Benson to all other young men I had ever known.

"Your future is very bright with George as your husband," she told me. "You could never find a finer, truer, more honest and intelligent young man as your life companion. I feel so satisfied, darling child, to know that some day you're going to marry him."

She paused, then added with emotion, "Promise me, dear, you will never see Arthur again." Then she broke down and started crying, and I began to cry, too. "Mama," I said, "I'll never see him again. He's gone out of my life. I wouldn't hurt you for anything, because I love you more than the whole world put together."

"I want you to go to college before you marry," she went on, her voice still emotional. "I thought we could send you this fall, but times seem so hard. You must go next year, though. Promise me you'll wait to get married until you've finished college. Will you, dear? "

"Yes, mama, I promise."

Time slipped away fast while we were having this long heart-to-heart talk. Mama had been so upset in recent months about the house matter. There never seemed to be time for the two of us to have our long talks.

Mama and I had hardly finished our talk late that Sunday afternoon when I heard George's familiar footsteps coming fast as usual down the street to our front door. The board sidewalk ran along past the front of the shop. On the other side of the walk was a small irrigation ditch, like on all streets in Union. That irrigation water made possible, among other things, the beautiful big poplars lining streets all over town. George stayed for tea, and we spent the evening together in our living room, which opened into the back of the store. Mama was with us part of the time, but went into the store several times during his visit, though it was, of course, closed on Sundays.

Papa spent that evening across the street sitting on a

bench in front of Levy's dry goods store, talking with Mr. Leon Levy. He didn't seem to realize that since it was mama's birthday, she would want him with her. I felt anxious all the time about mama. I could see she was worrying over the bad feelings with papa about his wanting to leave Union, and selling our home, then mama's buying it back. Yet she tried to be cheerful. During much of the evening she talked and laughed with George and me. He left about ten o'clock.

Shortly afterward, papa came home. He was fond of George, too. Mama and I prepared for bed. We were always back and forth in each other's bedroom, chatting and fussing with our delicate skins. It seemed necessary for both of us to put on them the only thing we knew in those pioneer days: rose water and glycerine. We put mutton tallow on our lips and hands. The climate was so dry that our lips would crack and bleed. Mutton tallow rendered from mutton fat had a very softening and healing effect on lips and hands.

While we were looking in the mirror over the dresser in my room, as we often did, I said, "Mama, you don't look old enough to be my mother. You really do look more like my sister. Everyone says so."

"I'm getting along in years, Maudie, dear," she said. "But I'll try to keep young for your sake. But you have your life before you and I know it will always be happy. George is such a fine young man."

Then we kissed each other good night and she went to her room and I jumped into my bed. I fell asleep immediately and slept soundly all night.

When I awoke the next morning about six-thirty, the first thing I heard was low, deep voices, seemingly in our living room. Papa knocked urgently on my bedroom door, then opened it and stood in the doorway. When he spoke, his voice was choked with emotion and fear. "Maude, where's your mother?" An awful feeling of foreboding swept through me.

"Where's mama, papa? Isn't she there with you?" I became wild with fear. I could hardly struggle into my clothes. I sensed, like an animal does, that something terribly wrong had happened. *Why the talking out by our front door? What's the matter? Where's mama?* All this ran through my mind like bolts of lightning.

"She went to bed when I did," papa said, his voice breaking with emotion. "But I can't find her now."

I ran to him, crying and trembling with fear and anxiety and threw my arms around him. "Oh, papa! She must be here! She wouldn't go anywhere. Oh, mama..."

"She wasn't in bed when I woke up a few minutes ago," he said. "Come see if you can find her anywhere about the place." I hurriedly went into the kitchen and back yard, calling her. There was my big gray cat at the kitchen door, wanting in, as usual. So mama hadn't opened the back door, as was her daily custom, being the first one up. I was getting nearly hysterical. If mama needed something from the store or butcher shop for breakfast, she always called me to run the errand.

I ran screaming back to papa, who was now walking toward the store to check there for her. Papa was crying, too, and could hardly talk. I heard several voices on the sidewalk outside the front door of the shop. Then one of the men, a family friend, burst into the shop and called to me, "Maude, you and your father come out here and see if this can be your mother."

I was paralyzed with fear. I could hardly walk out the front door. Oh! The terrible sight I then looked upon. Mama was lying on the sidewalk just beyond our front door, where several men, family friends, had moved her.

"Oh, yes," I wailed, shattered, "it's mama." I kneeled beside her. "Mama! Speak to me! Oh, speak to me!" I looked up to papa and the other men. "Can't somebody do something for mama? Bring back my mama. She can't be dead! Oh, no! no!" I screamed. Then I fainted, still kneeling there.

The men friends had found mama's body lying face down in the shallow irrigation ditch that ran along the outside edge of the sidewalk in front of the store. The water was only four or five inches deep. Poplars grew just beyond the edge of the ditch. Her head was near one of the trees. Her face was in the shallow water when they found her, and her hands were tied behind her with a face towel—tied in a secure double knot that would not come loose.

When I came to, I was lying on my bed. Some of mama's and my dearest friends were rubbing my hands and face with camphor. I couldn't focus my thoughts at first. Why are all these people here? Soon my mind cleared. Then the awful realization flooded through me. Mama is gone. Gone forever from papa and me.

"I can't give her up. I can't. I can't...." I kept saying over and over. I asked them all to try to bring her back. But they gently explained that she was beyond help.

Papa was prostrated, too. Several of his men friends had made him go to bed, then remained nearby. Several ladies came and took care of me. They thought it best for him not to come to me just then because of the added grief of our being together. I was so grief-stricken I couldn't even see some of mama's best friends, like Adelia Stewart and Mrs. John Wright. I couldn't remember what happened from then until three days later when I heard the ringing of the Methodist Church bell. It was tolling for mama's funeral.

"I can't stand to hear the bell..." I said, breaking out in fresh crying. So friends had the minister stop it. I had not been able to leave my bed since the tragedy and was too distraught to attend the funeral. I wanted to get up and go, but mama's friends said no, it would be best for my recovery not to. The only time they let me see mama again was when she had been brought into the living room dressed in her shroud, looking so natural and beautiful lying there in her casket.

Mama was gone from us by her own efforts; it seemed incredible but true. She had managed somehow to tie her hands behind her with the towel. How could we ever know why she did that terrible act that broke our hearts—carried away the most precious thing in our lives? And she left no message. The whole town was in mourning. All business houses closed. Poor papa was at the funeral—the only living family member present. My first meeting with my chums and mama's dearest women friends nearly killed me. They all cried, and my grief welled up even more.

During the funeral service, our dear friends, the Warren family, took me to their home on the edge of town, where they had a small ranch and a nice, big home. Lora and Sally Warren worked for mama, learning the trade. Mrs. Warren—Aunt "Mug" we all called her—was waiting for us. They put me to bed in the guest room downstairs. I remembered very little for days afterward. The first impressions I had were the quiet feelings of my surroundings. Then I was aware of Lora and Sally and George Benson sitting by my bed. They began to talk about things that might take my thoughts away from mama and the funeral, and to stop me from trying to solve the terrible mystery of my mama's tragic end.

Finally, to give me a change when they wouldn't let me go home to papa, Sam and Lora Benson, George's brother and sister-in-law—just like a brother and sister to me—took me to their home for an indefinite time. They and Mother

Benson and George kept me there a long time and did everything they could for me. As the days passed, papa came more often to see me, and my closest chums were allowed to start visiting me. George came every day on his way to work. He now worked for the County Clerk, Turner Oliver, who once was George's and my school teacher. George also came every evening. He often brought me boxes of candy, flowers, or some little favor. To keep my mind off my loss, Sam and Lora taught George and me to play whist. I often held lucky hands and became interested in the game. George's and my engagement had not been publicly announced yet. The whole town seemed to know, though, since he had given me a beautiful blue-white diamond engagement ring.

I kept thinking about why mama took her own life. It happened in a time when many businesses were experiencing hard times that caused her some worry. She carried a large stock of merchandise. Winter was coming on, when business was usually much slower anyway. But that couldn't be it. It didn't seem to bother her much.

There was the strong tension related to papa's wanting her to move to Portland. But she had bought our house back, even though we hadn't yet moved back into it. She hadn't been able to brace herself to confront him about it and insist on moving back into our house.

I loved my father and he loved me, but I can never remember even sitting on his lap or his kissing me or caressing me, except on leaving or returning home. He was always rather dictatorial and severe with me, and he was exceedingly careful and particular in my early training.

In the past month or two before the tragedy, papa was not at all demonstrative toward mama. In evenings he seemed to prefer the company of men, sitting with them across the street on dry goods boxes, talking and whittling—never dreaming that mama longed for his companionship and affection of former days. It was that attitude of indifference in papa she could neither stand nor understand. Besides that, I believed that all mama's and my recent good talks, including her great satisfaction over George's and my engagement— knowing now that I would be well cared for in the future— pointed to the sad conclusion that she had premeditated the taking of her own life.

Several papers, including one in Union and one in Portland, carried stories that said mama could never have tied her hands behind her, and in a hard double knot the way the towel was tied. Others, including all her friends, said no one did that awful tragedy but mama, herself, and she wasn't insane but in her right mind when she did it.

When the Union editor made the former statement, papa, as soon as he read it, walked over to his office and gave him a beating. I didn't blame papa and stood up for him through it all, for I was positive of his innocence. He, like me, had gone through all he could stand, and there was no one else who could have murdered her. I know God must have forgiven her, and I hope she has found more happiness and contentment in heaven.

Grandma Knowles became prostrated at the news of mama's death. When she recovered sufficiently, she wrote and asked me to come and stay with her. She said she needed me. I didn't want to leave papa and George. I felt papa needed me, and George didn't want me to go. He had been so very kind and good and thoughtful to me all through my great sorrow. Papa felt I should not try to live in our family home again, and I'd be too upset at mama's store—each with all those memories.

While papa liked George, it was obvious he didn't want me to marry him, and probably was encouraging me go East to break up the school days love match. I can't remember ever in my life having sat down for a heart-to-heart talk with papa. Now, I gave papa my word I'd go to Grandma Knowles and agreed further, upon his strong urging, that I would study art. Some of my school friends had said over the years that they thought some day I should study art. Papa suggested the Art Institute of Chicago.

"Maude, please don't go," George pleaded. "It might be for years. It might be forever. You might meet some swell city chap and never think of me again. If we don't marry, I'll never marry anyone else. But I can win the world with you by my side." He asked me to marry him before leaving.

When I told him I couldn't marry him and then immediately be separated from him, he asked me to marry him secretly. No one else would know. Then in a year he'd come to Illinois and we'd visit the World Fair in Chicago and travel around some through the East on our honeymoon.

"If I go East," I told him, "I'll return within a year. I want to come back and live here."

In the end I decided to go. When George drove me to the station in his buggy, he was still trying to get me to change my mind. He said he could soon have a nice home fixed up for us to live in. I was almost persuaded. But then I remembered my promise to papa, and grandma needed me. Also, there was often in the back of my mind the feeling that while I did think the world of him, I wasn't sure I actually loved him enough to marry him. Finally, I did want to study art. The Oregon Short Line finally whistled its departure signal. George and I bid a tearful goodbye. In minutes the station was out of sight.

When the train pulled into Petersburg, Illinois five days later, there were good old Grandpa Knowles and one of my girl friends, Mary Bradley, from my earlier visits, to greet me. We drove seven miles in grandpa's buggy to his farm in Greenview, which I knew so well by now. I found poor grandma sick in bed from the shock of mama's death. I felt grandma really did need me, for after grandpa, I was now next in her affection. She was feeling much better a month later, and soon began having as much company as she used to. She and grandpa loved to entertain.

After several more months, when grandma was pretty much recovered, I talked with her and grandpa about my desire to enter the Art Institute. She finally reluctantly gave her consent. It was clear that she thought Chicago was a big, wicked city and could hold great danger for a little country girl like her granddaughter. She got my friend, Mary Bradley, to promise to go with me to Chicago, 170 miles away, to help me get safely settled. Mary had recently married and her husband was well off, so she could easily afford the trip. Never having been to Chicago, she quickly agreed to go with me.

Grandma set one other requirement for my going to Chicago. I must write to Mr. and Mrs. Tom Connelly, whom she said mama knew well, and ask if I could board with them. So it was arranged with Mrs. Connelly and her husband, a professor at one of the schools on the north side, near the lake. Mary and I were very excited when the day of our departure came. Grandma Knowles and some of our young friends saw us off at the railroad station.

I never even dreamed of the experiences lying ahead of me in Chicago that would shape and change the rest of my life so greatly.

Chapter XV

Student Life At the Art Institute

The Connellys met Mary and me at Union Station in Chicago when the Illinois Central train pulled in. They immediately recognized us two green country girls. Instead of taking us directly home, they asked the carriage driver to go to Sherry's—one of the swankiest restaurants in Chicago in the 1890's. This was Mary's and my introduction to big city life. A liveried doorman welcomed us and, inside, the headwaiter, in formal clothes, greeted us cordially and led us across the thickest carpeting I had ever walked on. We followed him past table after table of elegantly dressed people to a place for four in the center of the dining room.

As soon as we were seated, Mary and I began to look around and were captivated by what we saw. Ornate crystal chandeliers reflected in many mirrors on the walls. This effect was enhanced by bright electric lights everywhere. The air of excitement they created, along with the animated voices of people at tables all around us, the fine linen tablecloths and napkins, delicate glassware and sterling silverware, was a heady experience for two small-town girls. Glancing at the Connellys, I was certain they saw and were enjoying our overwhelmed reaction to our surroundings.

How surprised the other diners would have been had they known that the green young lady from eastern Oregon, more at home in a western saddle than on one of these plush chairs, had at that moment a loaded pistol—a six-shooter—in the velvet bag on her lap. George had given it to me shortly before I left, to defend myself from any danger, he said. I had gone hunting in Oregon many times with papa and George, so I knew how to use a pistol and a rifle.

In the previous few weeks, Mary and I had discussed several times our forthcoming visit to wicked Chicago. Surely in such a city, we both believed, danger lurked. What would a girl do if someone tried to lure her into danger? We had the impression that this might happen to us at any time on the streets—even in broad daylight. We decided it was prudent for me to carry the pistol. What we didn't know was that it was against the law to carry a concealed weapon. No town in eastern Oregon had any such restriction. In the days that followed, however, we saw all was going well. There appeared to be no danger and no need for a pistol, so I quit carrying it. Mary returned home after a nice visit for a week around the city.

The Connellys lived in north Chicago, about three blocks from Lake Michigan. She was a fine, motherly woman, somewhat stout and very jolly. Mr. Connelly was an equally fine person. They took so much interest in me that I soon felt comfortable in going to them for advice in all my doings.

In early January, 1892, shortly after my arrival, Mrs. Connelly went with me to the Art Institute when I applied to enroll in the full Art course. The school was then located in a five-story, dark red stone building facing the lake. On every floor were wide galleries. Beautiful statuary seemed to be everywhere. Pupils had pitched their easels all over the galleries. Some easels were right in front of statues, and new students were busy sketching them, as their first lessons in drawing and shading in black and white.

After completing enrollment, I was told my first class would begin the next morning. I was so excited that I couldn't sleep that night. I could hardly wait to write papa and George all about it. My first class was in one of the galleries. I felt a great air of exhilaration as I looked around at my fellow students and their easels. I thought, now at last I'm taking my first steps to become a professional artist. The studies proved to be an effective diversion from my sorrow, for I had to concentrate fully on them.

I gradually became well acquainted with a fine group of young women and men around my own age who kind of adopted me. I believe this was partly because they visualized Oregon as the Wild West. During lunchtime and other shorter breaks they often gathered around me and asked me to tell them about the cowboys and Indians and other aspects of life in eastern Oregon. They seemed genuinely fascinated that here among them was a girl who actually had traveled across the plains in a covered wagon, lived on the frontier, knew about horses and ranch and village life.

I soon began getting invited to parties and banquets at the Art Institute. But living so far from the school, I could not always attend, nor did I even wish to do so at night. I had home studies. Often, too, I sat up late at night writing letters to George Benson, my chums, and dear papa. Many times, despite the glamour of the Art Institute, I'd get home-sick and begin to think about mama; then I'd cry myself to sleep.

From the start I loved my studies and applied myself faithfully. After being there about two months, I was promoted to the Antique class with honorable mention. As soon as I became well acquainted with some of the girls, they asked me if I had met Mr. Vanderpool, the head art instructor, whom they described as a wonderful artist. They said I must meet him, because every student who knew him liked and admired him greatly. One day several girls took me to meet him. I was nervous.

"Oh, yes," he said after the introduction, "I have been criticizing Miss Summers' splendid work in the galleries."

I had not yet learned the names of all the Art Institute faculty. Now I felt very happy to meet the head instructor. After that, he always seemed to show strong interest in my work. Next, I was assigned to the Still Life class. It became one of my favorites.

By now, the Connellys had moved closer in toward the Art Institute and took a nine-room apartment in a very attractive part of the city. They did this partly in preparation for the Chicago World Fair, to open in 1893. They planned to rent several spare bedrooms to roomers during the Fair. They now told me I could have company from the Art Institute any time I wished.

I began walking to and from school, over the State Street bridge. But on very cold winter mornings the freezing winds off the lake would give me a pain in my chest. On such mornings I rode in the carette: a large sort of bus, drawn by two lovely big draft horses. But too often those fine, willing horses would slip and slide around and fall on the ice-crusted cobblestones. I always felt so sorry for them, thinking of our own beloved horses, King and Sparkie and Charlie, and my pony, Dexter.

One day I heard from several classmates that Mr. Vanderpool wanted me to pose for him. First, he asked two other girls to try to get my consent. I refused. I said it would take time from my work. Beyond that, I had never modeled before and knew nothing about how to do it. Then one day after class Mr. Vanderpool spoke to me.

"Won't you please let me paint a picture of you, Miss Summers? If you give your agreement, I will help you make up any lost time in your work."

I finally agreed to pose for him. It had been difficult for me earlier to turn down this top artist among the faculty, who had a reputation as one of the best of all Chicago's artists. It turned out to be a fascinating experience, with some mystery involved.

He told me he wanted me to pose for a life-size oil painting, to be completed in time to enter it in the annual Charles T. Yerkes Chicago artists competition. The prize each year was $500.00. In 1892, that amount represented a lot of purchasing power. I was uneasy about the matter not only because of my complete lack of experience modeling, but also because I felt papa might disapprove of it, and I wasn't at all sure George would agree to it.

Mr. John Vanderpool was a Hollander. He was of small stature, with a slender build and very broad shoulders. He always wore a Van Dyke style beard which gave his face an angular look. His large brown eyes reflected exceeding kindness, and they often seemed to project an air of sadness. Perhaps that was because he had a pronounced back deformity which, some other student told me, he'd had from birth. Yet most of the time he was very cheerful and sometimes jovial. He had recently married a beautiful young lady, a former student at the Institute.

Part of his work as chief art instructor included teaching

the Life class. All the students considered him a superb teacher. I was grateful to him for taking time with his critiques of my drawing and shading work and, later, paintings. He never passed my easel without stopping to offer helpful suggestions.

I told Mr. and Mrs. Connelly about his wanting me to model for him. To my surprise, they congratulated me and a few days later gave a little party for me. They said they were proud of my progress at the Art Institute and for being picked as the subject of a painting by such a distin-guished artist as Mr. Vanderpool. After that, I was somewhat surprised to find that I was invited to attend even more Art Institute dinners and parties and, through staff members there, to join several clubs. It began to be a gay life. I was wearing George's beautiful diamond on my ring finger, and I was always careful to let young men who showed special interest in me know that I was engaged.

On the appointed day, I went to Mr. Vanderpool's studio in a lovely, large, old-fashioned residence set back from the street on Michigan Avenue. Many artists had their studios in this old building with its front of white stone. A wrought iron fence with a fancy gate surrounded the lot. As I rang the bell, I wondered if I was doing right in going to his studio alone and posing for him. I also wondered again how George would take it. After all, since I was engaged to him, he ought to have something to say about it. When Mr. Vanderpool opened the door and greeted me, I imme-diately felt much more at ease.

He said he wanted me to pose sitting in an Episcopal church pew, wearing all black clothes and a turban. I was always dressed in black then because of mama's death. He wanted me to have a gold-headed umbrella by my side and hold an open prayer book on my lap. Some days later he said he wanted much of my reddish-brown hair to show underneath my turban. After I began the modeling, another faculty member told me it was partly my fresh, wholesome look, unassuming country ways, and my girlish complexion, with so much natural rich color from outdoor living, that appealed to Mr. Vanderpool. As the painting progressed, I could see the black clothing accentuated my color and the red in my hair.

At first, as he painted, I was nervous and my neck grew tired. Modeling can be hard work. But he was understanding and allowed short rests, sometimes with a cup of tea or a glass of milk and a sandwich. Usually I posed two or three hours in the afternoon. Sometimes one or another faculty colleague dropped by to chat or read to us while he painted. When the painting was finally completed, Mr. Vanderpool was all smiles. He told me he felt it had turned out exceedingly well, and he had high hopes it would win.

The night of the big awards reception, I was dressed, at Mr. Vanderpool's request, in the same clothes I wore for modeling, and had with me the umbrella and prayer book. The Connellys and some of their good friends were among the invited guests, too. The painting, now in a beautiful gold leaf frame, was displayed in the most prominent location, perhaps because of Mr. Vanderpool's high reputation as an artist.

During the reception, people would look at me and then at the painting. Some asked me to stand beside it, so they could compare it better. I began to enjoy every minute of it. I was delighted to hear other artists and critics rave over the wonderful likeness and beautiful effect Mr. Vanderpool had created.

Finally came the highlight of the evening. The moderator introduced the judges in front of the large gathering of artists and guests. With much ceremony, including a dramatic pause, they announced the winner. Mr. Vanderpool's painting was awarded the coveted Charles T. Yerkes prize!

While there was much celebrating that night, the next morning was like a funeral. Some hours after the reception ended, the top floor of the Atheneum Building was deliberately set afire by someone. Every painting in the Yerkes exhibit was destroyed in the blaze. Some artists even lost their studios in the building. Many of Mr. Vanderpool's friends and associates expressed their belief the next day that some competing artist, envious and greatly disappointed that his own painting hadn't won, started the fire. Examinations by fire experts indicated there could have been no other cause.

We were all very upset over the loss. Mr. Vanderpool took it as a tragedy. He had declared the painting to be his masterpiece. I saw tears in the corners of his eyes.

"I'll gladly pose for you so you can paint it again, Mr. Vanderpool," I told him the morning after the fire.

"Oh, Miss Summers," he said, "it's wonderful of you to say that. It was my best painting. But I just haven't the heart to paint it again. I couldn't paint it again like I did the first time. One cannot paint a masterpiece twice."

In the days that followed, I looked forward strongly to the chapel services. While there, my cares slipped away for a while. It was very restful and renewing. I had always attended some church—usually the Methodist—and I loved to sing the old familiar hymns. Mama and papa had sung and taught me many of them during our covered wagon travels. Most students attended chapel. One girl I began attending with once in a while in the spring was Maud Maple. Several months earlier I had been in the office and seen her name on some list. "Maud Maple," I read aloud, then looked up at the instructor I was there to see. "That's a very nice sounding name," I said.

"Yes, and she's a very nice girl. I must introduce you to her soon," she responded. We became acquainted a few days later. During the spring term, Maud Maple and I became very good friends and spent much time together. She said she wanted me to go home with her sometime for a weekend, and her mother had agreed. So when Easter Sunday was near, she asked me to spend that weekend with her and her family. We left the Art Institute together on Friday afternoon for her family home on Campbell Park, in one of the Chicago residential areas.

This was the beginning of an experience that was to bring about another major change in my life.

Chapter XVI

Life With the Maples

After classes on the Friday before Easter, 1892, Maud Maple and I rode together on the horse-drawn streetcar to her home. Mrs. Maple, a very friendly, cheerful looking lady, greeted us at the front door of their nice, big house, then led us into the back parlor. There I met Mr. Maple, just home from work, and Maud's younger sister, Grace, who was eleven. Mr. Maple seemed a little more formal than his wife but still pleasant and friendly. After the introductions, Grace volunteered that her brother would be home soon. While we visited during the hour before supper, I found myself relaxing and becoming at ease with the family.

After a while their Irish maid, Mary, came in and told Mrs. Maple that dinner was ready. The table was set for six, but the chair opposite me was empty, because the brother, Will, hadn't arrived. Mrs. Maple rang a little silver tea bell when she wanted Mary. During the dinner there was more lively talk, including many questions about my life out in

Oregon. Afterward, Maud and I spent much of the evening playing the piano and singing popular songs of the day. Gracie listened and tried to sing along with us. I was curious to meet the brother, but I never saw him that evening.

The family helped make my weekend a happy and memorable one. On Sunday morning at breakfast Mrs. Maple told us that Easter dinner would be about one o'clock. We were all sitting in the front parlor around noon talking and having a good time when Maud's brother walked into the room. As she introduced him to me, my first impression was how handsome and lively he looked and sounded. He immediately joined in the spirited talk, which flowed unbroken right into the dining room with us.

Again there were questions about my life in Oregon and our covered wagon experiences. The family seemed fascinated to be talking with someone with such a background. This sounded like the Art Institute parties all over again. I was never quite sure whether the Maples and my friends at the Art Institute regarded my different background as a privileged one: colorful and high adventure, or that of a "hillbilly" from Oregon's mountains and plains. I felt very secure in the matter. I thought it was a good, solid background. I was even a little proud of it.

Sitting around the table, I saw that Gracie, with her blonde hair and large, dark blue eyes, favored her mother. Mrs. Maple's hair was dark blonde—somewhat graying, which made her eyebrows look darker and quite attractive. Will also favored his mother more than his father. He had her large, dark blue eyes and fair complexion, but his hair, slightly wavy, was a rich, thick, light brown. He looked very fit and stood six feet tall. Maud looked more like her father, with dark brown hair and lighter blue eyes. Mrs. Maple almost always had a happy expression and seemed serene and unruffled. She was witty, with a gift of being able to make people laugh by the way she could effortlessly put a little twist on words. Her son seemed to have inherited some of her disposition. Mr. Maple was more serious. Maud told me that her brother was about my age—nineteen—and that he didn't work yet.

Will excused himself late in the afternoon and left the house. Not long afterward, two nice looking young men who were the Maples' near neighbors, dropped in. Maud and I had a jolly time visiting with them. Mrs. Maple invited them to stay for supper. About ten o'clock Sunday evening the two young men, Maud and I, were still singing at the piano when Will walked in. Soon he joined us. The next morning Maud and I were off for the Art Institute early enough to make our first classes. Before we left, Mrs. Maple invited me to come back and spend more weekends with them.

All the time I was at the Art Institute, papa was in the Territory of Alaska. He had left Union not long after I did. He loved Alaska and the life there and had a modest degree of success in developing a couple of little mines. While he sent me money to live on, sometimes it was a long time between checks. It wasn't his fault. He was in remote villages, and it could take months for mail to get from a village to a seacoast town, where the steamer would carry it down the coast to Seattle. He said my letters also took a long time to reach him.

Twice he sent me a sturdy little wooden box filled with small gold nuggets, just as he had found them in the mines and streams. From time to time he wrote articles for newspapers and magazines about life in Alaska. He was up there for several years, and when he did return, he had a yearning to get back up North.

Maud Maple told me one day not long after my Easter

weekend visit with her family that her brother Will said to her, "Sis, why don't you have Miss Summers come again? She's the only one of your Art Institute friends you've brought home who has really impressed me."

Maud and I continued to spend a lot of time together at school, often comparing notes on our sketching and painting classes. At mealtimes we often relaxed by telling stories of some of our lighthearted experiences and laughing over them. We grew to be close friends. Meantime, I was studying hard in the Still Life class. Occasionally I posed for Mr. Vanderpool and for the Sketch class on Saturdays. I spent several more weekends that spring with Maud and her family.

I wrote to Grandma Knowles at their farm and to papa's twin sister, Aunt Lydia, living not many miles from them, that as soon as school was out in June, I'd come to them for the summer. Meantime, Maud told me one day her family really liked me and they invited me to come and live with them. George still wrote nearly every day, and wanted to marry me as soon as I finished my art course. I told him I planned to spend a second year at the Art Institute. Since the Connellys were planning to move away from Chicago soon, I happily accepted the Maples' invitation to live with them at 29 Campbell Park during the next school year.

I was going to miss the Connellys. They had been like my own family to me. They couldn't have been nicer. The Maples gave me a warm welcome to their home one early autumn day when Maud and I came there together with my bags from the Connellys. Again I joined them in their little custom of sitting and visiting together in the back parlor during the quiet time before dinner. This was always followed by more lively talk at the dinner table. After a few months, I felt like I was becoming a part of this delightful family, much as I had with the Connellys. They all seemed genuinely pleased to have me there, which in turn, made me feel at ease and happy to be with them.

For entertainment, families in the Maples' neighborhood of Chicago, anyway, did some of the same things we did back in Union. Sometimes two or more families got together for dinner and to play card games such as Whist, Euchre, Five Hundred, or Cinch. Quite often on weekends Maud would invite a few young men and women around our ages from the neighborhood over for the evening to sing together or play cards or both.

Sometimes we'd all go ice skating on a pond in a nearby park. Maud and I got exercise in good weather by walking home from the Art Institute, since their home was only three miles from the school. Chicago at this time had few cable streetcars and even fewer electric ones, all of them operated only inside the Loop: the business district. Public transportation to residential areas was by horse-drawn little streetcars, which were very slow.

Directly across the street from the Maples' home at 29 Campbell Park was the Baum family: Frank, the father, who was more than six feet tall, his wife, four young boys, and her mother. Frank Baum was then working for Marshall Field in Chicago. Years later I was interested to learn that he became nationally famous for his fairy tales such as *The Wonderful Wizard of Oz, The Land of Nod,* and many other delightful stories for children.

Mr. and Mrs. Maple mentioned to me several times in my first two months with them how happy they were that my being there seemed to help keep Will home more at night. I'd noticed, too, that he was staying home more, but I didn't know I had anything to do with it. He was home for dinner most of the time now. The parents and Maud did everything they could think of to encourage this change. The family, sometimes joined by neighbors, played card games more often, and board games like checkers and carom. Sometimes they got hold of some good stereopticon slides and put on a little show at home.

Maud and I joined a neighborhood card club of young people. We finally persuaded Will to join, too. He and I had many good times together at those card games, often winning as partners. We usually sat at the same table when refreshments were served.

One evening while the family and I were sitting around the front parlor telling stories, I described how, during the year I stayed with Grandma and grandpa Knowles, a boy I got to know quite well began calling me Ethel, because he thought it was such a pretty sounding name. Will picked right up on this.

"Ethel. Ethel... I like that!" From then on he began to call me Ethel and gradually the rest of the family and their friends around the neighborhood did, too. It suited his sister and me fine, since there were two Maud(e)s in the home. Anyway, I always thought Maude is a rather plain name.

That winter of 1892 at the Maples' home was a happy time of family evenings and weekends together. Maud and I joined them on weekends and on week nights when we didn't have homework. Much of the time we did have to study at night. Will loved to sing, and he had quite a good voice. He always stood at Maud's left side while she played the piano and I stood at her right. As the weeks went by, he began more and more often to give me amorous glances— especially when we were singing love songs. Among his favorites—all popular in those years— were *Annie Rooney*, *After the Ball*, and *In the Gloaming*.

I began to see that Will was falling in love with me, and I didn't want this to happen. I was very careful not to flirt or encourage him in any other way. I always wore George's engagement ring, and I often talked with the family about him, always in very complimentary terms.

One Saturday morning while he was helping me do breakfast dishes, Will told me he was growing awfully fond of me. Then he said, "Ethel, don't you think we'd make a good pair? I'd like to be with you always."

I stopped him short and reminded him that I was engaged to George Benson. A few weeks later when we were having a heart-to-heart talk, he asked me if I couldn't give up the Oregon fellow and quit wearing his ring. I told Will I like him very much—like a brother—but I couldn't think of doing as he asked because I didn't love him. I asked him to stop any more talk of that kind. I must have sounded pretty firm, because he looked so hurt and downcast afterwards. But that only stopped him for a few weeks. I realized more and more that I was finding him very fascinating and was increasingly enjoying his devoted attention.

Will had gone about a year to Lombard College, where his father once studied law, but he didn't find it to his liking and dropped out. Mr. Maple was a lawyer and real estate investor. He owned a considerable amount of rental property. He tried to get Will to join with him at the office. For a while Will worked for his father on the real estate side, but he really did very little work and you could tell he wasn't interested enough in real estate work to make it a career.

He continued his ardent attentions to me. My life was getting too complicated. Here I was engaged to George Benson, with plans to be married when I finished art school. Yet I felt attracted more and more to Will. I decided with much reluctance that I'd leave the Maple home.

After I told the family that I'd be moving out soon, things went on about as usual. I thought Will didn't believe

I'd really leave. He often would say things like, "I'll stay home if Ethel is going to be here," or "I'll play cards if Ethel will," and "I'll go to the store if Ethel will go with me." Sometimes I'd do those things to please him and help keep him at home. His lighthearted manner and humorous ways made me feel good to be around him, and we did a lot of laughing together.

In late winter I completed my current course at the Art Institute. Then I carried out my decision to leave. I could tell that both Maud and Will were genuinely surprised that I had really meant it when I said I was going to leave. I decided to return to Illinois to spend some time with Grandma and Grandpa Knowles and papa's twin sister, Aunt Lydia and Uncle Milem. I needed to get my thinking straightened out.

Chapter XVII

I Make the Biggest Decision of My Life

It felt very good to be back with my relatives. First, I spent some time with Grandma and Grandpa Knowles. They welcomed me warmly, but they didn't ask me much about the Art Institute. Aunt Lydia kept urging me to come over to their place for a week or two. I said I'd come soon. While staying with my grandparents, I made several day or overnight visits with my good friend, Mary Bradley, who had helped get me safely settled in wicked Chicago when I first went there.

For weeks while at grandma's and grandpa's farm, I was invited out to dinners, suppers, and parties, by old friends from my earlier visits and by many of my relatives' friends. After one visit with Mary and her young husband, Henry, she drove me in their fine buggy over to Petersburg to stay a while with Aunt Lydia and Uncle Milem. Again, there was lots of company coming and going.

One day when Aunt Lydia and I were alone, I opened

my heart to her. I told her about George Benson and just how I felt about him. I talked about his fine character, steadfastness, how much he seemed to truly love me, and how mama loved George and thought I was going to marry him. Then I told her all about Will and how he wrote to me now almost daily, and in every letter he asked me to marry him.

I told Aunt Lydia how, against my own instincts, I had grown to love him and that before I left their home I had allowed him to kiss me. And now I felt more attracted to him than to any other young man I'd ever met.

She listened, absorbed, to all of this. As I talked, I had a strong feeling that Aunt Lydia was showing in her whole being that she loved me deeply and wanted the best for me. When I had finished, she looked intently into my eyes and spoke very earnestly.

"Maudie, do you think he'll be a *good provider*? That's the main thing to consider if you love a man. If a man's not a good provider, a woman can't live with him. I really believe from all you say that you love him. And you don't ever want to marry a man you don't love.

"I've never thought, Maudie," she continued very seriously, "that you cared enough for George to marry him. And I believe you really love Will. You never seemed crazy about any of the other boys you've gone with like you seem now about him. I wish I knew him better so I could advise you. But if you love him and he can provide for you, I'd say he is the choice. Consider it all very, very carefully, dear, before you make your final decision. You're kin, and I want to see you happily married."

She was really the only one I could turn to for advice in reaching this most important decision of my life. I knew she would be as honest with me as with her own daughters.

In those days, the thing young ladies thinking about marriage heard all the time from their mothers and fathers and others who counseled them was, *"Is he a good provider?"*

That part of the advice came as no surprise. But her advice left me with one part easy to answer: I loved Will without any doubt in my mind. But the other part about whether he'd be a good provider, I couldn't answer as confidently. He was now only twenty-one and hadn't yet found his niche.

Following my talk with Aunt Lydia, I spent many nights tossing and turning and losing sleep over the prospect of not fulfilling my pledge to mama about marrying George. My anguish became almost unbearable when I thought of breaking my engagement with George—the loving, upright, kind and sensitive young man that he was. This became even more difficult, if possible, when I thought of his letters, in which he poured out his plans to come to grandma's and grandpa's to marry me, take me to the Chicago World's Fair, and then take his "beautiful artist bride," as he frequently put it, back to Union. There he had bought a home and personally furnished it lovingly. I could imagine how heart-broken George would be.

But I knew I loved Will with all my heart, and nothing else seemed to matter. After going over and over these thoughts night after night, I often ended up crying myself to sleep. The day came when I reached a decision. I would marry Will. I wrote him and said I had broken my engagement with George Benson and that I loved only him. He wrote back, elated, by return mail. He wanted us to get married immediately.

Answering his letter, I said in very plain language that he was unemployed and could not keep a wife. But if he would get a good position and work steadily, then we could talk about getting married.

Will had his father go with him immediately to a jewelry store to select an engagement ring for me: a clear, blue-white diamond in a solid gold narrow band. I was very happy and proud to wear it.

After I wrote to George, he answered with a terribly sad letter. He told me to keep the ring and do as I wished with it. His letter made me start crying all over again, and that lasted for days.

When the Maples' dear next door neighbor, Mr. Edward Walker, learned that Will and I were engaged, he got Will a fine job with the Chicago, Milwaukee and St. Paul Railroad as a car inspector at the Union Depot. Now Will's letters carried a strong sense of urgency about his desire to get married immediately.

Aunt Lydia wanted a big wedding at their home, and so did my grandparents at their farm. Will suggested we have a quiet church wedding. This appealed immediately to me, since it saved choosing between my grandparents' or Aunt Lydia's place. Besides, I had a limited amount for my wedding clothes and other expenses. My close girl friend, Mary Bradley, agreed she and her husband, Henry, would stand up for us. And they invited us to spend our honeymoon at their nice farm home.

So that's how it was all arranged. The wedding date was set for April 8, 1893, in Petersburg. After leaving Aunt Lydia's for another visit with my grandparents, I returned to stay with Mary and Henry until the wedding day. I wrote to papa in Alaska. I didn't know it then, but he was in the process of moving back to Oregon and taking up a forty-acre farm near Roseburg. He didn't get my letter for many months.

There really had been very little courtship between Will and me. Girls seldom did any "petting" in those days. If they did, they were ostracized by their friends. I'm sure Will thought more of me because I was so particular, for he was naturally very modest. While I was at their house, the only times he ever had his arms around me were those two or three nights the week or so before I left, when I let him kiss me. We had seldom even been alone together except when sometimes just the two of us went ice skating or took walks in the neighborhood. Our courtship had been mostly in the front parlor when he and Maud and I sang together.

It was arranged that Will would arrive by an early train on the Saturday morning of our wedding day. Mary and Henry and I drove in their surrey to the depot to meet him. On our way to the station I was very quiet. After a while Henry said. "Why so quiet, Maude? Aren't you happy?"

"Yes, I think so," I answered.

"Maybe you better wait if you feel that way—if you aren't absolutely sure," Henry said. Then I began to cry, and I didn't know what I was crying about.

I know I love him," I said with strong confidence.

The train rolled in and there was Will. I have to this day engraved in my memory the most vivid and precious picture of him at that moment. I saw the handsomest young man, with grace, an aristocratic air of a millionaire, and he looked so self-assured and happy. He was dressed in a dark, well-tailored suit, wore a light felt fedora hat, and he carried in one hand a swell gentleman's grip—small suitcase.

"Oh, Maude!" Mary said, bubbling. "Isn't he handsome!"

"I love him! I'm crazy about him!" I said, suddenly overflowing with happiness. No wee voice could possibly have stopped me now. This was our wedding day!

After warm greetings all around, we piled into the surrey and Henry drove us to Petersburg. Will and I sat in the back seat. He was in high spirits and seemed to enjoy the trip immensely. Soon he had me feeling the same way.

The wedding ceremony, which took place about noon at the minister's home, was very short. The only others present were the minister's wife and Mary and her husband. Then we four left for the best hotel in town, where we had a fine dinner. Afterward, we drove to Mary's and Henry's farm, where they had arranged a big wedding reception and supper, with lots of our mutual friends and relatives invited. We had our honeymoon at their farm until the next Tuesday, when we took the train to Chicago.

The Maples greeted us warmly. Mrs. Maple seemed especially happy to see me back—now as Will's wife. Tears came into her eyes as she kissed us both. We moved into Will's room on the second floor.

There at 29 Campbell Park I began to be a much closer part of the Maple family. I felt this new relationship with the rest of the family almost immediately, and I liked it very much.

The first evening Will came home after a day at work, he took me in his arms and said, "Oh, the joy of coming home and finding you here waiting for me! Could there be anything sweeter?" As long as he worked during our married life, he often said things like that to me.

Sometimes in that first year I'd walk down to Will's office and he and I would go out to supper and occasionally to a show. When he talked to me about his long-term career interest, the one thing that made his eyes really light up would be when he confided that what he'd like most to work toward was to some day become a railroad train engineer. His father was interested in politics. He often asked Will to go with him to political meetings downtown. But he soon saw that his son had no interest in politics, so he stopped inviting him.

After we were married, I gradually gave up my Art Institute friends except Maud. On some weekends Will and I went skating at one of the parks in the winter. In spring and summer we'd have a lot of fun riding a bicycle built for two, a gift from his parents. We rode it all around Chicago's suburbs. I'd get so hungry and thirsty on those trips. I was always glad when he suggested stopping at some little cafe for refreshments. He always had a cold beer or two and urged me to try a beer, but I never cared to.

That first summer and autumn, Will and I had so much fun wandering around all over the Chicago World Fair grounds. There were huge, happy and excited crowds. The sound of music, usually within hearing distance wherever we were, the tantalizing fragrances of cooking food, and the endless variety of new things to come, made it all a delightful place for both of us. Fair exhibits that Will particularly enjoyed were the engines and new mechanical inventions.

We were surprised to read late in the summer that the great Chicago World Fair of '93 was, despite the big crowds, losing money. Newspapers said that this was due partly to the fact that the financial panic of '93 was beginning to take hold. Many in the Fair crowds must have been, like Will and me, taking in the free things and spending modestly. As times got harder, more and more people began walking the streets of Chicago and other parts of the nation looking for work.

About seven months after we were married, I knew I was pregnant. When my time came, the delivery was complicated because the baby was quite large. At first the doctor said the baby couldn't live because it would be too difficult to deliver. A little later, he said he'd try to save it. In those days, nearly all women had their babies at home. Mine was born in an upstairs bedroom at the Maples' house, with the family doctor in attendance and Mrs. Maple hovering around, doing all she could to comfort and otherwise help me.

The doctor saved my baby, all right, but the instruments he used in doing so damaged my insides. For a while, the doctor and family weren't sure either the baby or I would live. Getting ready for and during the delivery, Will was wonderful. He was at my side the whole time, holding my hand whenever that was possible.

Our baby, a very healthy boy, was born on June 26, 1894. Will and I named him William Summers, after Will and both grandparents. From the beginning he thrived and grew.

The Panic of '93 dealt a heavy blow to real estate values. Many people whose property was heavily mortgaged lost everything. Mr. Maple didn't believe in taking big risks, so his properties didn't carry big mortgages. Still, he was forced to sell several fine big houses and a few prime vacant lots located in nice residential areas for far less than they were worth only a year earlier, in order to keep up payments on the rest of his properties. Now the Maples were not nearly as well off; still, they could manage to live very comfortably, and they did.

During those early years of our marriage, we lived at first with Will's parents. Will's sister, Maud, got married and moved with her husband to Missouri. Mr. and Mrs. Maple adored and enjoyed spending as much time as they could with their new grandson. He enriched their lives as well as Will's and mine.

Our second child, Alpheus Fuller Maple, was born at 29 Campbell Park on May 29, 1902. He also was a fine, healthy baby, who thrived from the start. We named him for Mrs. Maple's favorite brother, who lived on the south side of Chicago. Uncle Alphy, over six feet tall, like all of Mrs. Maple's brothers, worked his way up from laborer to a high level position with the Burlington Railroad Company.

While Will's parents liked to have us with them, Will and I had decided to rent a nice five-room apartment not too far away and lived there for more than a year. But as the depression got worse, Mr. Maple suggested to Will that we move back in with them and share expenses. We agreed to this.

We had found being in our own place was very attractive; yet when we moved back in with his folks, it seemed to me like coming home. Once again we became a close part of a loving family. With all of Mr. Maple's side of the family and all of hers, along with my family in Illinois and papa near Gold Beach in Oregon, we now belonged to quite a large and mostly joyful clan. And so the years sped by.

Will and I often agreed that the biggest thing in our lives and our finest legacy were our two sons. Looking back over the years now, and having had the privilege of watching our sons grow to young manhood and follow their destinies, I am certain of it. I want to take brief note of them.

Chapter XVIII

My Legacy

Looking back over the years from when I traveled with my parents on the Overland and Oregon Trails, until now, as I finish writing this in the early 1940's, I find the time has gone all too fast. Will would quickly agree that our greatest legacies are our two children: happy, smiling, eternally good-natured Summers—our first-born. And there is Alpheus, with those same fine qualities, and also with a very strong spirit of adventure in him. Both boys were equally bright and able, each with so much promise for a successful, fulfilled life. But fate stepped in. Summers' star was crossed when he was still a young man. Alpheus went on—goes on—with a full, rich life, and much promise for his years that lie ahead.

As a boy, Summers was always cheerful, happy-go-lucky, thoughtful and generous. He was such a good big brother to Alpheus—"Alphy" we called him when he was small—who was eight years younger. By the time Alphy was a grammar school boy, his father was unable to be with either boy. Summers stepped in and did all he could to help his younger brother have a fine, happy boyhood. He probably didn't think of it that way, but he helped Alphy learn many things boys growing up in those years might have learned from their fathers. If Summers was going on a bicycle outing on a sunny day, he'd take Alphy along on the bar just in front of him. As soon as Alphy's legs were long enough, Summers taught him to ride a bike. He took his kid brother on fishing and duck hunting trips, and camping in the summertime. And he made certain his little brother learned to swim. He was always looking after Alphy.

Alphy was a boy with great curiosity and wide-ranging interests. He clearly was born with a strong creative aptitude. So I began to teach him to sketch and paint. In a few years he was on his way to becoming a fine artist in several media—particularly oils. It became one of his strong life-time interests.

When the Germans and the Allied forces fought each other in World War I, Summers followed the newspaper reports intently. Family radios were still a few years away. As soon as America entered the war, Summers volunteered, joined the Army and went to France. We worried about him day and night. Although he survived and returned home, he had been badly gassed in a big battle with the Germans.

At first, upon his return, he looked fairly normal and felt somewhat well. Anxious to get back to civilian life, he didn't accept the opportunity to have extensive Army medical rehabilitation treatment at Fort Sam Houston, offered to soldiers who had been gassed. This turned out to be a very costly mistake on his part. The effects of the gassing began to cause severe disfigurement and a slow, relentless deterioration in his general health. He went out to the area around

Gold Beach, Oregon, where grandfather John Summers—my own father—had developed a prune orchard in later years. But my son's life has lost much of its quality. Because of his disfigurement, his former high spirit and outgoing personality have been dampened. He has felt the pain of being shunned by some who might otherwise have been friends and neighbors.

Alpheus was much more fortunate. In 1918, at age sixteen, and unknown to me, he marched down to a Navy recruiting station and enlisted. He never left the states while in the Navy. A fine student from his primary years onward, he accepted, after the war, a scholarship at the University of Chicago, and later studied at several other universities.

Alphy seemed to have almost an instinctive love for horses. When he was in his early teens, I taught him to handle horses in harness, and he did very well. He did quite a bit of riding while he was at the University of Chicago. He took advantage of the opportunity to ride Army horses whenever he found time. After his college years, he continued to ride.

Early in his career, Alpheus became a trainee with Shell Oil Company, which led to executive-level positions. While with Shell Oil, he became fascinated with airplanes, and learned to fly in an open-cockpit biplane in the late 1920's. That was a time when aviation was still in its infancy in the United States.

An example of his spirit of adventure was his acceptance of an offer by another pilot with whom he had become acquainted—a former World War I flyer—to deliver an open cockpit monoplane to its new owner in California. Knowing that Alpeheus had only a student pilot's license, his aviator friend said he would act as navigator and would teach Alpheus cross-country flying.

They picked up the plane at Hagerstown, Maryland.

My son flew it to the West Coast. He told me that in 1932, when they made the transcontinental flight, there were no aerial navigation aids. When pilots in their open cockpits encountered rainstorms, lightning, or other bad weather conditions, they had two choices. They could look for a place to land, though there were very few airports then, or accept the brunt of the elements. They completed the trip without difficulty.

Through his flying interests while still with Shell Oil, Alpheus became acquainted with Jimmy Doolittle, who gained fame in World War II for his raid on Japan. He flew with Doolittle on at least one occasion before the war. They became life-long friends.

At Shell Oil, he showed a strong interest in writing, sometimes combining it with his sketching ability, to do articles for the company's in-house publication for their distributors, dealers, and the Shell Oil staff. Mostly he wrote for them on aviation subjects. Later, he was assigned to handle aviation affairs in the office of the company president. While handling this assignment, he wrote and illustrated a scholarly article on the highlights of aeronautical engineering and pioneer American aviators, including Jimmy Doolittle.

His work at Shell Oil later led to offers, by the owners of the Ziff-Davis publications, of top positions with both *Popular Photography* and *Popular Aviation* magazines. He accepted. He became the first Managing Editor of *Popular Photography*. When he first went to *Popular Aviation*, its contents were devoted to people interested in making model airplanes. He was given major responsibility for transforming it to a general interest aviation magazine.

Still later, he and a businessman who was a close friend, decided to start their own import business. They became the U. S. distributors for Swiss Bolex products, including the

well-known Bolex cameras and Hermes typewriters. But
when World War II came along, Alpheus turned the business
over to his partner and took an important assignment related
to the war effort. He accepted a position with Pan American
World Airways as chief of construction on a contract with
the U. S. Army to build a series of airfields across Africa,
badly needed by the British and other allied forces to fight
the Germans and Italians in Africa.

Best of all, both young men married truly wonderful
young ladies: Summers' beloved Kathryn and Alpheus' precious Jean Layer. In making this biggest and most important
decision of their lives, they have often said they couldn't have
done better. I fully agree with them.

While I have written much more about Alpheus than
about my dear son Summers, it is only because Alpheus has
had the good fortune to live on with brimming good health
to utilize much more fully his talents, and he continues to
do so. Summers is equally talented, but the bad effects of
his wartime experience have cut short his opportunities to
use them more fully. I am just as proud of Summers, who
laid his life on the line for his country.

Yes, as Will and I have often said to each other, the
biggest thing in our lives and our finest legacy are our two
sons. Looking back, watching them grow up over the years
to fine young manhood in that pre-World War I era is another
whole story—much of it part of a vanishing way of life. But
this is the place to close my pioneer days story.

John Colon Summers, father of Maude Summers Maple

Mary "Mollie" Reynolds Summers, mother of Maude Summers Maple

Maude and William "Will" Maple, summer of 1895

William Summers Maple, older son of Will and Maude Maple, 1909, at age 15.

Maude Summers Maple, taken about 1915

Brothers Summers and Alpheus Maple have a postwar reunion in 1919.

Colonel Alpheus F. Maple, A.U.S. (Ret.), 1946;
son of Maude and Will Maple.

Downtown Denver about 1870

Photo courtesy Colorado Historical Society

Denver residential area about 1870
Photo courtesy Colorado Historical Society

City of Denver about 1870
Photo courtesy Colorado Historical Society

Green River, Wyoming, about 1880.

Photo: Sweetwater Historical Society, Green River, Wyoming

Rock Springs, Wyoming Territory, early 1880s.
Photo: Sweetwater Historical Museum, Green River, Wyoming

Salt Lake City, Utah Territory, from Arsenal Hill, about 1882.
Photo courtesy Utah State Historical Society, Salt Lake City, Utah

Photo courtesy of Carbon County Museum, Rawlins, Wyoming

Rawlins, Wyoming, in late 1870s.

Photo courtesy of Carbon County Museum, Rawlins, Wyoming

INDEX

A

Almquist, Leonard, v
Art Institute of Chicago, 120, 121, 124, 125, 130, 134

B

Baker City, V, 71
Bannock Tribe, 59
Basket Socials, 96-97
Baum, Frank, 135
Bear River, 56-58, 57
Beef Cattle, 22
Benson, George, 95, 105-108, 112, 113, 117, 120, 134, 137, 140-142
Benson, Jennie, 105
Benson, Lora and Sam, 117
Boise, 59-61
Boles, Frances, 13, 15
Bradley, Henry, 139, 142-144
Bradley, Mary, 120, 121, 123, 139, 142-144
Buffalos, 19, 47, 48

C

California, 37, 58
Camping, 107
Campsites, 39, 47
Carter, Mable, 88, 103
Carter, Miles, 108
Chavers, Lou, vi
Cheyenne, 10, 16, 17, 21
Chicago World Fair (1893), 120, 125, 145
Chinook winds, 68
Chores, 31, 40, 57, 82, 89

Church, 82, 92, 106, 112, 116, 129
Clayton Ranch, 16
Colorado, 4, 15
Columbia River, 59
Coffinberry, Mina, 81, 105
Connelly, Mr. and Mrs. Tom, 121-123, 125, 127, 134
Continental Divide, 35, 36
Cows, 7, 38, 69
Coyotes, 56
Customs, 23, 76

D

Denver (1878), 5-10
Divorce, 95
Doolittle, Jimmy, 151
Dowell, Lydia, 98, 102, 134, 138-142
Dowell, Mollie, 98, 99, 102, 105

E

Electricity (Union), 96

F

Ferries, 25, 28, 54, 61
Food, 55, 60, 67, 68
Fort Boise, 60, 61
Fort Hall, 58-60
Fort Laramie, 21
Fuel (campfire), 19, 40